Write for the Fight
A Collection of Seasonal Essays

by

Tess Hardwick and Tracey M. Hansen

Together with eleven other writers

Gordon Bonnet, Galit Breen, F. Jo Bruce,
Derek Flynn, Jesse James Freeman, Laura Kilmartin,
Marni Mann, Karla J. Nellenbach, Terry Persun,
Laura Tiberio, Laura Zera

booktrope

Booktrope Editions
Seattle WA 2012

Copyright 2012 Tess Hardwick and Tracey M. Hansen

This work is licensed under a Creative Commons Attribution-Noncommercial-No Derivative Works 3.0 Unported License.

Attribution — You must attribute the work in the manner specified by the author or licensor (but not in any way that suggests that they endorse you or your use of the work).

Noncommercial — You may not use this work for commercial purposes.

No Derivative Works — You may not alter, transform, or build upon this work.

Inquiries about additional permissions should be directed to: info@booktrope.com

Cover Design by Greg Simanson
Cover Image Copyright © 2010 Bea Thompson

Edited by Diane Hughes

Special arrangements and pricing may be available for bulk purchase by educational or charitable groups or other organizations. For further information please contact info@booktrope.com.

EPUB ISBN: 978-1-62015-047-4

Print ISBN: 978-1-935961-43-7

Library of Congress Control Number: 2012933612

Table of Contents

Why we Write for the Fight
Introduction: Tess Hardwick   7

Part One: Spring
What do you miss about being 5 years old?   11

Tess Hardwick	12
Gordon Bonnet	16
Galit Breen	19
F. Jo Bruce	21
Derek Flynn	24
Jesse James Freeman	27
Laura Kilmartin	30
Marni Mann	33
Karla J. Nellenbach	36
Terry Persun	39
Laura Tiberio	42
Laura Zera	45
Tracey M. Hansen	48

Part Two: Summer
What would you tell your 20-year-old self?   51

Tess Hardwick	52
Gordon Bonnet	55
Galit Breen	58
F. Jo Bruce	60
Derek Flynn	63
Jesse James Freeman	66
Laura Kilmartin	69
Marni Mann	72

Karla J. Nellenbach	75
Terry Persun	78
Laura Tiberio	81
Laura Zera	85
Tracey M. Hansen	88

Part Three: Autumn
What, at this point in your life, do you want, wish and dream of for your life going forward?   **91**

Tess Hardwick	92
Gordon Bonnet	94
Galit Breen	96
F. Jo Bruce	99
Derek Flynn	103
Jesse James Freeman	105
Laura Kilmartin	108
Marni Mann	111
Karla J. Nellenbach	114
Terry Persun	117
Laura Tiberio	120
Laura Zera	123
Tracey M. Hansen	126

Part Four: Winter
What would you want said about you on your 80th birthday?   **129**

Tess Hardwick	130
Gordon Bonnet	134
Galit Breen	137
F. Jo Bruce	140
Derek Flynn	143
Jesse James Freeman	146

Laura Kilmartin	148
Marni Mann	151
Karla J. Nellenbach	153
Terry Persun	156
Laura Tiberio	158
Laura Zera	161
Tracey M. Hansen	164

Some closing thoughts

Conclusion: Tracey M. Hansen   164

Contributors   170
    Gordon Bonnet
    Galit Breen
    F. Jo Bruce
    Derek Flynn
    Jesse James Freeman
    Tracey M. Hansen
    Tess Hardwick
    Diane Hughes
    Laura Kilmartin
    Marni Mann
    Karla J. Nellenbach
    Terry Persun
    Bea Thompson
    Laura Tiberio
    Laura Zera

Introduction – Why We *Write for the Fight*
By Tess Hardwick, co-author

The year was 1999. I was 30 years old, newly engaged and looking forward to the next phase of my life. I worked with a team of a dozen human resources professionals at a young high-tech company. I remember vividly a staff meeting, all of us gathered around a large conference room table. I don't remember the work discussed that day, only the faces of my colleagues. Most of us were in our late 20s or early 30s, and all of us were in the throes of life: ambitious, driven and dripping with vitality.

Our team leader, Julie Aydelotte, was a little over 40 with school-aged children and stories of growing up on Lopez Island and working on commercial fishing boats off the coast of Alaska. I've always said she was the toughest woman I ever met, even though her appearance was more of the supermodel variety, tall and slender with beautiful, thick brown hair. Several months into our working relationship, she was diagnosed with breast cancer. A month later, I watched helplessly as strands of her lustrous brown hair fell out in clumps on First Avenue and drifted toward Puget Sound, carried away by spring breezes. After surgery and chemo, Julie went into remission. Several years later, we trained for a three-day cancer walk together. I thought she'd escaped. Years went by; she moved to Bellingham. One day, during a rare visit to Seattle, she met me for coffee in the lobby of my downtown office building. We toasted her remission, almost seven years by that point, and my second pregnancy. We said goodbye in the lobby, and when I got into the elevator, she remained, waving and smiling her gentle smile as the doors shut.

It was the last time I saw her. A little over two years later, she passed away after an aggressive form of the cancer came back, diagnosed just weeks after our final visit. I didn't even know she was sick again. She was private that way, and — as I'd suspected all along — tough, working up to the very end of her life. When I got the call from her daughter, a freshman at Sarah Lawrence, I knew. Julie was gone.

Another of us at that table, Jen Dynes, wrote to me several months ago. She'd just had a double mastectomy after getting the dreaded news, just months after her 40th birthday, that a tumor had been found in one of her breasts. It was her first mammogram. As we talked over the phone recently, I recalled the first time I ever met her. She wore a long denim shirt, hiding just a hint of a belly bump, pregnant with her first baby, glowing and beautiful; and another time, standing in front of my office with a mug of steaming green tea, touting its health benefits.

Then, there is my aunt, diagnosed at 57 and now in remission after a difficult year of chemo, radiation and medicine. There's television personality Giuliana Rancic who, like Jen, chose a full mastectomy. As I was putting the final polish on the essays for this book, I learned of a woman in her early 50s, here in my community, and my sister-in-law's niece, not yet 30, both passing from an aggressive form of breast cancer just days before Christmas.

These young women were all conscientious about their health, fit and strong. But cancer knows no boundaries, no rules. It is the universal equalizer. It leaves motherless children in its wake and friends and spouses who must figure a way to move forward into the empty space left behind by a woman they love.

It all leaves one feeling helpless, wondering what any of us can do to fight this disease. On my way to church one Sunday morning, I was seized, literally, with the idea for this anthology. Perhaps it was prompted by a fundraiser I'd recently attended, organized by my local Zumba teacher, Kelly Saunders, where we danced to raise money for breast cancer awareness and research. While driving that day, I envisioned the questions for the essays, organized as seasons to represent the different stages of our lives: spring, summer, autumn and winter. It seemed appropriate that a book celebrating and exploring the seasons of life was not only a great way to raise money

Introduction

but also in direct defiance to the disease itself. It was something, albeit small, to participate in this fight.

The essay questions are as follows:

What do you miss about being 5 years old?

What would you tell your 20-year-old self?

What, at this point in your life, do you want, wish and dream of for your life going forward?

What would you want said about you on your 80th birthday?

I'd heard an interview a few months before on Oprah radio with talented actor Rainn Wilson, where he asked Oprah, "What do you miss about being 5 years old?" I thought it was such a profound and beautiful question, and when I imagined this book, it came to me as a perfect question to represent the spring portion of our lives.

Asking what you would tell yourself at 20 is an idea I used on my blog, "Inspiration for Ordinary Life," that morphed into a weekly series featuring guest writers.

The question of your current wishes and goals, interestingly enough, was the most difficult for most of us to write. I suspect because it's the most revealing.

The 80-year-old question is often asked in leadership seminars and by life coaches, because it is an excellent way of informing your present choices. I thought it appropriate for our uses as well.

My hope is that after reading our essays you might contemplate the questions for yourself and perhaps write answers to a few or use them for group discussions at your book clubs and other gatherings. I suspect the answers will be as illuminating and clarifying to you as they were to us.

All essay contributors answer each question, organized by seasons. We've included biographies for each writer, as well as our cover artist, Bea Thompson, and editor, Diane Hughes, in case you want to know what other work we've done.

I chose my partner, Tracey Hansen, like I do many things: through pure gut instinct and in a flash. I'm an admirer of her work and talent, not to mention her raw, unbridled love of life. I also thought the juxtaposition of our voices would be interesting in an anthology. I was thrilled she agreed to lend her energy, time and talent to this project. She is everything one could want in a partner.

Some of the authors were hand-selected by Booktrope Publishing; others we found through a contest submission. They are from all different parts of the world — one hails all the way from Ireland — and are of different backgrounds, faiths and ages.

Our editor, Diane Hughes, is a freelance writer and editor with years of newspaper experience. I'm grateful for her diligent work, keen eyes and knowledge of all things grammatical.

Our beautiful cover was designed and painted by my talented mother, Bea Thompson, an award-winning watercolorist from southern Oregon. When we told her the concept for the anthology, she immediately seized upon the idea of tulips representing the different stages of life.

Tracey and I are grateful to Booktrope Publishing, Katherine Sears and Ken Shear for sponsoring and supporting this book, and for assigning their most talented resource, Heather Ludviksson, to project manage a bunch of crazy writers.

I leave you with this.

When Jen Dynes told friends of her diagnosis, they inevitably asked, "What can I do?"

"Get your mammogram," she said.

Yes, that. Please.

Spring

What do you miss about being 5 years old?

By Tess Hardwick, Co-Author

IN THE SPRING, WE LIVE on The Reservation in Hoopa, California. The house we rent has light blue siding, and all around us are brown-skinned friends with shiny black hair and eyes like cups of coffee. They make necklaces from pinecone beads and weave baskets to offer us as gifts.

My mother is young and beautiful. She has thick brown hair that she sometimes wears in a loose ponytail at the back of her neck and black glasses that make a curve at the sides. When she walks, the muscles of her calves are like camel humps. One day she surprises me with cardboard boxes she has cut and painted avocado green to make a pretend kitchen. I play next to the blue siding under my bedroom window; the sun is warm on my head. My mother paints at her easel with a brush in one hand and another between her teeth. Sometimes she steps away, her brows knitted in concentration, to study her work. Then she moves closer, dabbing and stroking until something recognizable emerges.

I am content.

My dad looks like the men on television in the toothpaste commercials. When he smiles, it's like the sun appearing. Before dinner, he plays music on the stereo, chosen from the records that lean against one another like the side of a roof. He holds them at the edge with both hands and knows how to aim the hole perfectly onto the metal rod. After he carefully places the needle on the record to avoid any scratching sound, the record spins around so quickly the words on the label blur into a streak. Dad doesn't allow me or my brothers to touch the records; we are only allowed to listen. The music streams from the speakers, and I believe there is a man inside who looks like a leprechaun and sings to us. There are no hindrances to my listening or my pleasure. I listen intently until I know every note and word.

Spring

In the mornings, my dad wears a tie and goes to work at the school where he teaches. On some evenings there are school events, and I get to go with him. His students are big children. They make a fuss over me, and I feel special because my dad is a teacher — someone who is respected and intelligent.

At the end of the summer, we're moving to Oregon. "To a house of our own," my dad says. The way he says it, I understand this is something wonderful. Between periods of packing, we swim at the river. My mother wears a two-piece bathing suit and sits on a rock with her feet in the water as she holds my baby brother. Her tanned skin is hot when I lean against her, and she smells of everything and anything I could ever need. Dad plays a game where he says he has a frog in his hands, but when I come close, he squirts me with water. We play this game again and again. Each time dad holds out his hands, I'm certain he has a frog — and I don't want to miss it. Each time, I get squirted — but I don't care. It's worth the risk.

In August, we pack all of our things into the car and truck. I'm delighted, because it's decided I am to go with my mother in the car, our ginger-hued Jeep Wagoneer. It's so loaded with boxes there is room only for me to join my mother. My brothers ride with my dad in the yellow truck. I feel grown up; I have my mother all to myself.

Our new house has a different smell, that of a wood-burning fireplace and something I can't name but begin to think of as the previous owners. The carpet is orange and brown. "Long shag," my brother informs me in a tone that conveys this carpet is special. I run my fingers through the orange and brown strands. I understand we're lucky to have this new giant house and fancy carpet.

I have my own room with purple flowers on the wallpaper and a purple carpet. There is a window that looks out on the front yard. Another girl lived here before me, my mother tells me. That girl is grown now, but I can still feel her and imagine a young woman with long yellow hair wearing a pink dress. Someday I'll be a lady and have long hair and pretty clothes and high-heeled shoes. I'll go to college. Maybe I'll be a teacher or a doctor or someone who writes books. My heart expands as I think of the possibilities, anticipating all that life holds for me.

There is a patio in back of the house, along with trees that have bark as thin as paper; it crinkles and folds into something that looks like a cinnamon stick. When no one is looking, my brothers and I pretend they're cigarettes. My older brother is tall and thin and wise. He'll be in fourth grade at the new school. He's quiet and likes to spend time alone reading books or working on experiments. When we go places, he likes me to talk because I'm the best talker in the family. My little brother is only 2. He's short and pudgy with a frame of straight brown hair that falls just above his eyes. I like it when he does what I tell him and holds my hand. I'm useful with my talking and hand-holding talents.

When the weather turns cooler — and the leaves on the trees fall, making a yellow blanket in the backyard — I go to school. Kindergarten is in the basement of a church. Our teachers are Miss Hillary and Mrs. Burch. But Mrs. Burch isn't there because she's been in a car accident, so Miss Hillary teaches us. She is young with light brown curls that hang by her shoulders; she speaks in a soft melodic voice when she reads us stories. After a month, Mrs. Burch is back. She's as old as Santa Claus and has short gray hairs that stick out on her upper lip and chin. She has a gravelly voice, and sometimes she yells because the children are naughty. I always follow directions. I do not want to get in trouble. My reward for paying close attention is that I learn to read.

At night, my mother works with me from sheets of paper with purple letters that smell of new paper and the ink from the copy machine I saw in the office. After a time, I realize nothing is better than curling up in the big green chair and reading to myself. I learn of Dick and Jane and their sister, Sally. I read about Spot and Puff. I'm smart like Jane — and pretty like Sally.

We visit the library. It smells clean and of books. There is a shelf near the front of the children's section with rows of stories I can read to myself. I can take home a whole armful of books, and it doesn't cost any money. This seems almost too good to be true. When I scan the rest of the library and think of all the books there just waiting for me to grow older and wise enough to read, I know that I am rich.

Spring

On Christmas Eve in our new home, the tree is lit with big colored lights and ornaments made by my mother. It grows dark outside, and frost forms at the edges of the sliding glass window. My father has bought a new Christmas record. In his perfect schoolteacher handwriting, he writes "1974" on the upper-right corner of the back cover. "We'll buy a new one for every year we live in our house," he tells me. My mother is in the kitchen. From the oven, there is a crackling sound and the smell of roast beef. There will also be gravy and mashed potatoes and homemade rolls that taste of butter. My mouth waters in anticipation. I know nothing of diets or guilt.

It begins to snow. I stand next to my father at the sliding glass door. He smells of his aftershave lotion and soap. In the light from the window, we watch the flakes fall from the dark sky until they land on our patio. Some meander, floating hither and thither, while others seem forceful in their descent.

"No two flakes are the same," my father tells me, taking my small hand in his. "We can't see it from here, because they're too small. If we had a magnifying glass, we would see they're all different."

I nod and sigh with pleasure. I am like a snowflake: perfect and unique.

By Gordon Bonnet

SEE THAT BOY, WALKING TO SCHOOL with his mom on the first day of kindergarten?
Sure, what about him? Looks like kind of a dopey kid. Thick plastic-framed glasses, bowl haircut, button-down shirt tucked into his shorts. Looks like he needs some serious fashion advice.
Hey, don't judge. Buddy Holly had plastic-framed glasses, remember? Maybe this little guy will grow up to be a rock star. You never know.
Yeah, maybe. But I doubt it. In any case, what's so special about this kid?
Just keep your eye on him, okay? He's got a long road ahead of him. He just doesn't know it yet.
So, why the big deal? What's your interest?
Some people just need watching. He's a little fragile.
Sickly, you mean?
Nah, not sickly. Physically, he's got the constitution of a horse. It's more of an emotional thing. He hasn't figured out that life hurts. He'll begin to realize soon, but it hasn't happened yet. He's still in that blissful space — a place where he'd probably choose to stay if he could, if he knew what was coming. It's the time before you know what life can do to you, hurting you, wounding and cutting. It's almost by accident sometimes, casually, like a guy brushing away a fly and breaking its wing, leaving it stunned and helpless on the ground. He'll find out soon; in three months or so, his parents will tell him that the family is moving back to Louisiana. That'll be the first thing, the first time he'll see that circumstances don't wrap you in velvet. The first time he'll get knocked down and have to pick himself up.
It's not such a big thing, moving. What does he see in this place, anyway? It's kind of dirty, this part of West Virginia. You'd think he'd be glad enough to leave.
It's change. He'll learn one good lesson and one bad from this; but good lessons never make the impression that the bad ones do. The good lesson is to appreciate what you've got, because it may not last; the bad one is to fear change, because change hurts. That more than anything.

Spring

How can we stop that? You sound like you already know what's going to happen to him.

Some. Not all. Maybe we can soften the blow a little, keep him from losing himself.

Sounds like he'll need some pretty powerful protection, if he's as breakable as all that. And we can't stop him from doing anything — or anyone else from doing something to him. You know it's against the rules.

You don't need to remind me of that.

Sounds like I did.

That's not the sort of help I'm talking about. What will keep him going isn't someone breaking his fall or keeping his knees from getting skinned. What I'm thinking about is passion.

A little young for that, isn't he?

Be serious. That's not what I meant, and you know it. I'm talking about passion for other things: music, nature, science. And words. Always words. He lives in the realm of language, and if he makes it, all his life will be spent talking, writing and finding new ways to say, "See this? Look at this! See it through my eyes. Hear it through my ears!"

Well, we can't give him those things. He's already got them, sounds like.

You're right; but we can keep them alive in him. This is the last moment, the very last moment that he will really believe that the people around him understand him, that they share his passion, that they understand how he sees the world. That vision can die — if he's convinced, somehow, that the way he sees the world is wrong. Thirteen years of public school will try to mold him into its own image — the model that takes children and forces them into cookie-cutter shapes. If it succeeds — well, he may come out alive, but what he was will have died.

It might be better for him if it did.

Less painful, maybe. Better? No. Never that. He will learn that he's different, and that will hurt. But at the same time, he'll discover that everyone is different, that conformity is one of the greatest evils, and that the best of humanity is found in the ways we differ from each other. It will hurt ... often. But better that than to lose the essence of himself.

People will ridicule him, you know.

Yes. That also begins today. The discovery that there are people who enjoy others' pain. One of the worst things of all. But even knowing that, if he can keep his voice, he'll survive.

It doesn't seem fair.

Life's not fair. A pity, but there it is.

He seems like a decent kid. I hope he makes it.

He is. And so do I.

Spring

By Galit Breen

I MISS MY CHILDHOOD, I think as full trees and bright houses give way to tall buildings and busy roads. Shades of blue and green melt by the windows.

The plastic seat is hard against my back; Kayli is warm by my side.

The smooth ride lulls my mind, heavies my lids. I glance at Kayli drinking in people and faces, languages and accents. Her eyes are serious, searching.

I am envious.

At her age, I rode buses and trains and subways in California and New York, Israel and Italy, Germany and England.

I memorized routes, grasped coins, planted feet and claimed seats. And then, I shared moments in time with strangers — a page out of our stories matched, a slice out of our days tethered.

I wove tales in my mind about these unsuspecting people. I'd lose myself in uniforms and scarves, briefcases and arguments. The stop, the details, the next steps — long forgotten.

So, yes, I miss my childhood. Not the singing and dancing, painting and playing, because as a teacher — and as a mother — I've tasted that sweetness twice.

What I miss is looking at people the way I did then, searching for their stories.

Today, Kayli leans against my shoulder. I brush my lips across her forehead and breathe in her apple-scented hair.

Above us, a robotic voice soothes stops and connections; green neon flashes towns, places, times. I breathe in these details, too.

I follow Kayli's eyes as I search for those stories, dig beneath those surfaces.

Ahead, a teenage girl with shimmering eye shadow and blushed cheeks laughs, her mouth wide and her silken curls swaying against the small of her back.

One eyelash flutter later, her friends turn away. She leans into the seat in front of her, rests her head, closes her eyes. She sits alone.

Farther ahead, the tall, middle-aged man who sat with his arms crossed and mouth set when we arrived has given up his seat for a mother and toddler.

The woman across from us has been speaking a titch too loudly for this shared space. She taps her impossibly high heel in rhythm to her meticulously painted nails.

Now she closes her phone, turns to Kayli and lilts to my girl about second grade and Magic Tree Houses, lip gloss and Katy Perry.

The train slows, and I glance out the window; I see a man stub out a cigarette before hopping on the train. His beard is matted, his T-shirt stained.

He sits down across from me; I avert my eyes.

Brody maneuvers into the space between Jason and me, reaching his suddenly long arms as he makes his way.

The train jars, and he loses his footing. That man whose eyes I wouldn't meet steadies him with the gentlest of hands and the kindest of smiles.

And now *I* am jarred. I'm seeing — really seeing — people and stories, faces and smiles, crisp lines and bright colors.

Shades of childhood run through my heart; words swirl through my mind. I crave to write.

By F. Jo Bruce

MY LIFE WAS MAGICAL at the age of 5. I was the "baby" of the family, with a brother and sister who were 13 and 10 years my senior, respectively. My family included one remaining grandparent —my granddaddy, who adored me — along with numerous cousins, aunts and uncles, and parents who loved and doted on me. But I'm sure they often wondered: "Where did this strange child come from?"

The year I turned 5 was 1952. Life was good in the post-war years. My family was lower-middle income and not without problems. We had hot heads, drinkers and some damned fools. We had good food and a comfortable house. My mother sewed lovely clothes for me. I was cherished, surrounded by love and protection.

What I miss most from that time is the total imagination I possessed. I still have it, but back then it was an airy, magical, mystical experience that came with emotion and total freedom. My imagination and mind were quicksilver, my body and mouth in constant motion, and everything could and did change in a twinkle of my black-fringed green eyes. I was a movie star in the heyday of Hollywood, trailing down our high steps with my mother's apron on backward (which made a glorious train). Then I would become a gypsy, a cowgirl, a mother with lots of babies, a (different) movie star, a theater usher, an elevator operator, a circus performer, another movie star (get the picture — no pun intended). My other roles included princess, fairy, nurse and someone named Aunt Hazel with a child's part played by my mother. Often I was a majorette — like my sister — with a stick for a baton. I usually had a scarf, an apron or various and sundry pieces of fabric tied on my head for long hair.

I miss the busyness of the life that went on around me. In the summer, the garden was very important to our kitchen and pantry. I didn't care much for going into the garden; bugs lived there! I didn't like bugs, was scared of every one of them and had a conniption fit when one got within sight of me. I loved helping my mama shell peas and beans and pulling the "hairs" off the corncobs. I had her practically undivided attention when we were doing this work. She sewed; I strung buttons. If she was in the kitchen, I was right there. I went where she went. I sat on my granddaddy's lap while he read. When I was tired, I would climb into my sister's lap, thumb in my mouth; she would rock and sing to me until I fell asleep.

We lived with my mother's dad. Her siblings and their offspring came to visit often. My mama cooked a lot, and I helped her. She made biscuits in a huge yellow Pyrex mixing bowl. I handed her the ingredients, talking a mile a minute as she mixed it all up with her hands, squishing the lard into the flour, pouring in the milk, watching it come out between her fingers. She pinched the dough off, rolled it in a ball, patted it into a biscuit and placed it on a large, greased pan. As she made each biscuit, she would name them after my uncles, aunts, cousins and siblings — even her and my daddy. This made me laugh. I stood on my stool beside her at the counter, and everyone was named *except ... me*. Sometimes she "forgot" to make me one, and I would have to excitedly remind her. Then she would make a small biscuit, which she had left a space for right in the middle of the pan. Next she would make an even smaller one, oddly shaped. This one she squeezed in right beside "me" and named it Trixie (who was our little terrier dog). How many times we did this I don't know. What I do know is biscuit making is one of my sharpest, happiest memories of being 5 years old. How I've wished I could go back there one more time, waiting, happy and excited as she began pinching off the balls of biscuit dough and naming them.

I miss hearing the big old school bus rattle down our road, stopping to disgorge my two cousins at their nearby home. I would run out to the stop at our drive and wait until the doors swung open for my beautiful sister to step off the bus. She would take my hand as I turned and waved the other one excitedly at my cousins, yelling "hellos" to them. Then out came my tousled-haired brother, who did his best imitation of ignoring me. I knew full well — and he knew that I knew — he had at least half of a soft, chewy rainbow-colored coconut candy plank or some big ole orange-colored marshmallow,

Spring

peanut-shaped candies in his pocket for me. The same thing happened every weekday, but I never failed to look forward to the school bus coming. I miss that ... always.

On some Friday nights, we had home football games; all of us went. My brother was on the fourth player string, and my big sister marched with the band as a majorette. She was beautiful ... and shiny. Her honey-blonde hair lay in soft curls below her shoulders. Her uniform was blue and white satin trimmed in gold buttons and braids. Over the short bottoms was a reversible circle skirt with a split — white on one side, gold on the other. Her short white boots had shiny tassels of gold and blue. Her baton would flash with the reflection of the lights when she was twirling it, especially when it was thrown high into the air. At the end of their routine, the girls unfastened their skirts, whipped them off and twirled them around over their heads like a bullfighter's cape while the band played behind them. That was my favorite part; I always jumped up and down, screaming and clapping my hands! I miss my excitement and those happy events.

My granddaddy brought me "sawdust curls" home from his small sawmill. The light-colored wood became fat blonde curls hanging from my jet-black hair. Blonde curls? Voila! I was Shirley Temple. I about wore out my black patent shoes on those days, tap dancing through the house, singing loudly. I've always missed my blonde curls and patent leather shoes, but only I missed my singing.

I miss the security, happiness and love, and the cocoon of protection I existed in. I miss most all the people whom I loved and who loved me. They offered security, brought happiness, taught important lessons, guided me and protected me. Most of them are gone now, leaving me here with my memories, which often bring smiles along with happy or sad tears. These memories wind themselves through the years in a soft gentle fog, rolling through my mind and heart, trickling from my fingertips onto paper.

By Derek Flynn

WHEN I THINK OF WHAT I MISS about being 5, it's not so much what actually took place but more what I felt at that age — and up to about the age of 12. During those years, there was a certain feeling that is hard to describe and that dissipates as the years progress.

That feeling was excitement.

Specifically, it was excitement over discovering new art — books, movies, etc. Now, don't get me wrong. This is not to suggest that new music or movies or books do not excite me still; they do. But there is a wondrous kind of excitement that only exists at that age, I think. And that is what I miss.

At the age of 5, everything is new. We see everything — every book, story, movie, TV show, piece of music — with wide-eyed innocence. We come to it fresh, our minds like a tabula rasa, a blank slate. We are unencumbered by the weight of pop culture that eventually builds up behind all these things and makes us a tad jaded and, dare I say it, cynical.

When I was a kid, I was a huge comics fan, but it was very hard to get comics in Ireland at the time. We got some of the British comics — Battle, Victor, 2000 AD — but there were no comic book shops here in those days, and the American comics were hard to come by. There was a sweet shop near my home that occasionally stocked the odd American comic book. (I later found out they were stacked into bundles and used as ballast for the ships delivering to Waterford. Any that survived were given to the local shopkeepers.) The offerings were random, and you would probably never see that same comic again. One month it might be an issue of The Amazing Spider-Man that ended on a cliffhanger with Spidey near death. How would he survive? Well, I'd never find out, because next month it would be an issue of Batman. And so it went. Not that it mattered to me. I pored over these comics like they were scripture. I read, reread,

Spring

then reread again. I looked at the ads for unknown and exotic American things, like Twinkies and Slinkies.

Nowadays, you can read comics online, and there are comic book shops dotted all over the country, so there's not the same excitement there once was in getting your hands on these rare gems. This lack of excitement is multiplied by the availability of things in the age of the Internet. Songs, movies, comics, books — all are available online 24/7. Spoilers for new movies and TV shows abound on the Internet. I remember watching *The Empire Strikes Back* as a young kid and finding out the shocking news that Darth Vader was Luke's father. Now we would likely find out that twist long before we ever went to see the movie. And I know I'm not alone in feeling that technology has spoiled the excitement. Filmmaker Kevin Smith (known for movies such as *Clerks* and *Chasing Amy* and himself a comics geek) expressed similar sentiments in an interview:

"It was an age of discovery ... sometimes, I wish I could go back to those days of waiting all week for a new book day."

That pretty much mirrors how I feel. And it's not just about comics. I remember listening to Bryan Adams' *Reckless* album (the one with *Summer of '69* on it) when I was a preteen and being blown away. It was one of the first times I'd heard — really heard — this type of guitar music. Of course, teens are notoriously fickle and time sensitive; within six months, Bryan was SO uncool, and I'd moved onto cooler bands. But for that six months, a sound came out of my speakers the likes of which I'd never heard before. This was how guitars were supposed to be played, and, someday, I wanted to play guitar like that, too!

But that's what being 5 or 7 or 10 or 12 is all about: discovering things for the first time and hopefully being inspired to go on and do something like that yourself — whether it's hearing music for the first time and wanting to be a musician or watching a plane take off and wanting to be a pilot. As we get older, and the "real world" encroaches on our dreams more and more, we tend to forget the excitement we felt in youth. Maybe we should try harder to remember what it felt like to be that kid, discovering those things for the first time and feeling that excitement. And maybe then we would realize that something else could be just around the corner ... waiting to make us feel like that again.

Spring

By Jesse James Freeman

I DON'T REMEMBER BEING 5 years old. I really never consider what I was like at such a young age, and I probably never would were it not for this writing addiction thing that my therapist can't seem to do anything about curing.

Turns out, thinking back, at the age of 5, I was on the edge. I was on a precipice and had no idea that I was. I was barely reading at 5 and hadn't gotten around to all those books yet that would change my life *cough* Joseph Campbell *cough.* I didn't have literature yet, beyond Spider-Man, to instill in me a love for storytelling. I knew that I could have it, though. There would be a lot of work to do, but the rewards seemed worth the academic challenge at hand. Plus, I was 5. It's not like I had anything better to do. I didn't have to run down to the coal mine every morning so I could pay the bills. (Thanks, Mom and Dad.)

All of the movies and TV shows and Atari that would play a major role in shaping who I would become were just being thought up when I was 5. Those things would begin to find their way to me, down that dirt road I lived on. Slow but sure — like molasses. They would soon begin the action of possession on my impressionable mind. I wanted more, though. I wanted into those books, and I wanted to devote myself to whatever they had to say. The signs were there. You could tell by the razzle-dazzle look in my eyes that there was no exorcist powerful enough to break the spell that stories and words were casting on me.

Every afternoon as she was calming us down after recess, my teacher used to read to us from Madeleine L'Engle's *A Wrinkle In Time*. I couldn't wait for story time every day. I would sit in my tiny chair, and when she began to speak, I wasn't in school anymore. I was transported across the universe with Mrs. Whatsit and a kid named Charles Wallace. I wanted to go with them — had to go with them. I had to know what was going to happen to us (well, them), but I also wanted to be able to tell a story like that, a story that could pull you in and make you forget about the real world. I wanted to write a story so intense that it could effectively enrapture a group of 5-year-old hellions who had just climbed off a set of monkey bars and run inside still filled with more energy than you'd need to open a Tesseract. I wanted to be some lady named Madeleine L'Engle who wrote books. (My therapist has mostly cured me of that. Now I just want to write books.)

I wanted to learn to read, and not just to make my kindergarten teacher start giving out gold stars. I'd already figured out all the Dick and Jane nonsense (well, the learning reading part of Dick and Jane). I knew there were worlds trapped inside those pages, and I took it as a personal crusade to storm the castle and take what I knew was mine.

I asked Santa for books, and I borrowed other ones. I'm pretty sure I even stole a few. I made people give me books that had all the hard words in them, the ones you had to sound out. There wasn't any "Hooked on Phonics" back then. It was the sink or swim days reading in front of the class; you either got a handle on it or got laughed away from the chalkboards.

This reading thing was turning out to be a lot harder than watching Godzilla movies on TV. I got the hang of it, though. I was able to add the written word to my box of ammunition, and it proved to be one of my better ideas. I had an overactive imagination that made books, and the stories within, fast friends. I began reading more and more and ignoring the TV and movies. It was much more fun to act out the adventure I'd just read about and build on that, making it my own thing. I did this often, and I did it loudly — much to the annoyance of the grown-ups around me.

I didn't have neighbor kids to pal around with when I wasn't at kindergarten. At the time it kind of sucked, but in 20/20 View-Master vision, it was great. I had to make up my own fun, and my only conspirator in all of this fun was my imagination.

Sent outside to play, I'd expand, re-structure and add to the tales of the fantastic that I was stacking up like Lego bricks in my head. I was posed with questions about a very strange world seen through the eyes of a very young child. I was coming up with my own answers for these questions in the only way I knew how — I was making stuff up. I was using the foundation that books were gifting me to build my own tower upon.

I had no clue then, but I was filling out the paperwork and taking the entrance exams to join the ranks of a long line of professionals who come before me. It was a great privilege: the chance to let my mind run wild and see where it would take me. I had plenty of stories to tell. The smiles on people's faces and the laughter and wonder I found I could invoke has ruined me ever since. I was allowed to be a kid, one who was constantly encouraged by parents, teachers and adults (who all loved books) to take my interest in books, storytelling and the adventure of it all to its highest level.

Jesse James: Kid-Shaman, Junior Nightmare. I let everyone know that I was going to learn to do what those author people did.

That's all I remember about being 5: books, reading and stories. Thanks to all who put up with me during that year when my imagination took hold and letters and words in strings began to make sense. Most of all, thanks for never dissuading or trying to perform that exorcism.

By Laura Kilmartin

AT THE AGE OF 5, I bitterly resented bedtime, believing it was nothing more than a ploy invented by adults to keep children from participating in the unknown (but certainly wondrous) adventures that took place after sunset. My parents spent more than one night carrying my sobbing self to bed because I viewed closing my eyes as an obstacle to wringing every possible moment of joy out of the day.

I dearly miss that 5-year-old child who begged, bargained and blackmailed for a reward no grander than the simple delight of a few more moments of consciousness to soak in life's sights and sounds. All I wanted was a temporary reprieve to read one more story, drink one more glass of milk or satisfy myself that Laura, Mary and baby Carrie would survive whatever peril they encountered that week on the prairie.

When I lost the bedtime battle, as I invariably did, I still refused to concede the war. I waited until after my jailers had tucked me in and returned downstairs; then I made my move. I crept to the quiet corner near the stairs, hid behind an oversized fern and eavesdropped shamelessly on the adult conversation below. I didn't always understand the topics being discussed, and I never attempted to participate (lest my hiding spot be discovered). But every moment spent cheating Morpheus' grasp felt like a victory.

Most evenings ended with a mad scramble for my bedroom after hearing my father click the television off and scuff his slippered feet toward the landing. I'd leap into my bed and pull the covers over my nose and mouth in an attempt to hide my pants of exertion and thrilling exhilaration at the thought of getting caught. Other nights would begin with me curled in my secret cubbyhole — straining valiantly to stay alert for just a few more moments — only to wake the next morning warm and secure in my bed with no memory of transitioning from one spot to the next.

SPRING

I miss having a hunger to live that is so deep and difficult to satisfy that one actually resents losing precious time to slumber. Somewhere along the way, that enthusiastic and obstinate 5-year-old was replaced by a woman in her 40s who spends most evenings glancing at her bed with a longing more appropriately reserved for a neglected but still desired lover. Today, the thought of passing up an opportunity to sleep is maddening, because there is nothing I crave more than a solid eight hours. But this goal is almost unattainable when balanced against work, bills, laundry, lunches and all the responsibilities a young child's mind cannot begin to fathom.

These days, once I finally do crawl into bed, the dawn seems to break before both eyes have had the chance to firmly shut. Not prepared to leave my comfy down cocoon, it takes the enticing scent of a pretimed coffeemaker and at least two rounds of uncoordinated batting with the snooze button to pull me kicking and screaming toward a new day.

I miss being 5 years old, when it seemed my body could sense the day had officially begun. My eyes would pop open, and I'd lie quivering under the blankets waiting for the magic moment when my mother would yell out to me, providing the permission I needed to spring from the bed and throw myself blissfully toward the unknown.

Each morning was a gift. Some were wrapped in a silver package with an elaborate bow, like those cold winter weekends when I awoke to a tray of cinnamon buns warming near the stove. Other mornings masqueraded as lumpy packages constructed of equal parts Scotch tape and Sunday funnies — but that didn't make them any less enjoyable. Those were the mornings I spent cross-legged on the living room floor in my daisy-print pajamas while consuming a bowl of soggy Cheerios. Raggedy Ann was tucked firmly at my side as we both watched Sesame Street. No one in my family could shake my firm conviction that Big Bird and Grover appeared to me — and me alone — for the sole purpose of explaining all I would ever need to know about the letter "S" and the number "6."

I feel lucky to retain my memories of being 5 but sad that their volume is muffled through so many filmy layers of years. The difference between remembering the joy of youth and actually feeling that same joy is much like seeing color in a black-and-white movie. On some level, I knew that Rosebud's namesake stencil was red, but as the sled flickers from my TV screen, it appears as just a richer shade of gray.

I may never again feel excitement for living as acutely as that 5-year-old who refused to go to bed, but from time to time I can remember, and then the colors in the world around me become much more vivid.

Spring

By Marni Mann

INSIDE THE MIND OF MY 5-YEAR-OLD SELF existed an innocence that was genuine and pure. I didn't understand why my neighbor's skin color was a shade lighter or darker than mine. I didn't notice if a house wasn't decorated with Christmas lights. I didn't find it odd if one of my friends had two mothers or two fathers. Words of hate and bigotry bounced off my little body. I didn't form an opinion until I got older and was capable of understanding the true meaning of those slurs. Life at 5 was light. Speech was heard and quite possibly absorbed, but the definition was unknown. The evilness of words — their power and how damaging they could be — wasn't a factor.

My parents made some decisions for me, but they also gave me options: which color shirt I wanted to wear for the school concert, what kind of sandwich I wanted for lunch, which sport to play during each season. My options fell into categories that had already been selected for me, but each choice not only helped mold my future but also challenged how capable I was to decide things on my own. My parents' job was to test me, to help ensure that I would make the correct decisions later in life. Whether I did or not was up to me, but they had built a foundation and taught me the difference between wrong and right. I miss when the biggest decision of the day was deciding between Fruit Loops or Special K, choosing a belly full of sugar or something more nutritional. A decision within one of my parents' preselected categories was much easier than a decision that would affect the rest of my life.

My mother dropped me off at school and picked me up. When I got home, I rode my bike. I didn't have a destination, and I wasn't in a hurry. When the neighborhood kids played flashlight tag at night, my team and I counted to 100 and then went to search the trees and decks of the surrounding houses. There wasn't a time limit. If we didn't find the kids before our curfew, we would look for them again the next night. Time wasn't managed; it was as unimportant as the weather. There wasn't a need to keep a schedule, worry about being late or feel the pressure of getting things completed on a deadline. I miss when time wasn't a necessity, when I didn't have to wear a watch and when the passing seconds didn't tick in my head.

When something hurt, I wrapped myself around the legs of one of my parents. I was then picked up into their arms and cradled against their chest. Within that comforting womb of arms and heat, my tears were absorbed into their clothes and a runny nose was wiped clean. The beating of their heart caused all other noise to fade into a whisper. Their words of love silenced my pain. I miss the warmth of their chest, how the pain was so easily dissolved and forgotten, and being just the right size to fit in their arms. I miss how miniscule those early heartaches were compared to the tragedy I experienced later in life.

My mother would wait for me to get into my pajamas and settled in bed before she came into my room. Even in the darkness, I could feel her presence: the swishing of her clothes, the smell of her perfume and her feet stepping over the carpet. She would brush the hair out of my face and tuck it behind my ears. Her lips would softly press against my cheek, and in her comforting voice, she would say, "Goodnight. I love you, pumpkin." She would leave my door open just a crack — enough to let in a stream of light. My dolls rested against the wall that touched my bed and in the open spaces along my headboard. I was never alone. I'd take one final look around my room, gazing at the wallpaper that showed pictures of each season and the shelf that held all the stories that took me into another world or time. Then, my eyes would finally land on the ceiling above my head, and I would make shapes out of the popcorn surface — just like I did with clouds in the sky. I would see horses and airplanes, and gummy bears the size of snowmen. Slowly, my eyes would close, and I would drift off to sleep thinking of the images I had created; they filled my dreams and kept me asleep until morning.

Spring

Thoughts and responsibilities didn't swirl around my head like a talking bubble. They didn't cause me to stir in the middle of the night or force my eyes to shoot open well before sunrise. At 5 years old, sleep was sound and uninterrupted, and I awoke rested. I miss that carefree existence.

By Karla J. Nellenbach

SOME OF THE BEST TIMES OF MY LIFE took place when I was 5 (or thereabouts). Let's face it, people. Childhood rocks the Kasbah. No bills. No job. No responsibilities to worry about — other than hosting the weekly tea party that is the highlight of your teddy bear's social calendar. Even better: When you're a kid, you can say or do just about anything — short of going on a multistate crime spree, which I'm pretty sure an adult or 16 might have something to say to your mom about — and get away with it because you just don't know any better.

So, of course, when some super-brainiac science geek finally constructs a working time machine, you can bet your sweet ass I'm reserving a spot on the trip back to 1984 to let the good times roll. And since I'm such a big fan of lists (aren't we all?), I'm going to throw out a little pile of things I loved so much as a tiny tot that I'd sell one of *your* kidneys to relive the glory days. (Well, of course, I wouldn't sell *my* kidney! Hello? I need it to, like, pee and stuff.)

1. Summers spent with my granny and gramps. My great-grandparents were the bomb. Granny taught me all sorts of card games and made the best root beer floats (with those heavy glass mugs from A&W that somehow ended up in her purse when we left the restaurant. Wink, wink.). And she always, always, always laughed at my jokes, even though I am *so* not nearly as funny as I'd like to think I am). Gramps was a crusty old man who was forever sneaking me packs of Doublemint gum and telling me that only wimps chewed one stick at a time. To this day, I'm surprised that all the candy and gum didn't rot the teeth right out of my head.

2. Making my mom read *Green Eggs and Ham* every night before I went to bed. Mom instilled within me a love of the written word very early on, and every night before my brother and I went to bed, we'd beg her to read us a story. Of course, she'd readily agree, then groan as we hauled out the beloved Seuss classic. It got to the point

where she'd read it so much that she only had to turn the page with no need to look at the book — she had the story memorized. I'm pretty sure she can still recite this story without missing a single word.

3. Annoying/tagging after my older brother. Unfortunately for him, as a child, I loved my older brother so much that I renamed him Buddy Josh ... because his name was Josh and he was my buddy. Duh. He *hated* it. He'd get so mad at me when I called him that, especially when his friends were around. And as most older brothers are wont to do, he'd resort to hair-pulling, pinching and general meanness to get rid of me. But I'd just keep coming back for more. Because he was my Buddy Josh. (Yes, eventually I stopped calling him that ... when I was like 13 or 14.)

4. My grandma teaching me to play Scrabble. When I was a kid, my grandma owned an ice cream shop where both my mom and my aunt worked. During slow periods, Grandma would get out the Scrabble board, and they'd all pass the time playing the game. After much begging and pleading, I finally got Grandma to let me play with her. Thus began a lifelong war we've waged over the board. When it comes to playing Scrabble, there is no such thing as family. It's a cutthroat business involving letter tiles, triple-word scores and the elusive seven-letter word. Grandma goes from being a kindly old woman to a sneaky cheater with no remorse for her actions. Just ask her about the great A-S-L-O debacle of 2003, and she will simply smile and say that it was my fault for not catching her misspelling of such a simple word as ALSO. That little stunt won her the game, and I still haven't forgiven her for it. As she says, "All's fair in love and Scrabble." Very true, Grandma. Very true, indeed.

5. Weekends at the ball field. When I was a kid, my dad belonged to a baseball league. Every Sunday afternoon, Mom would pack up a cooler, Dad would get his gear, and we'd all head to the baseball field where Dad and his team would go nine innings against a rival team. While the guys were playing ball, the moms would sit on the sidelines watching, and we kids would run off into the nearby woods and do some exploring. We'd spend hours running, jumping, slipping and sliding through the brush and back to the creek in the woods.

And when our moms called us back, we'd come running, covered in dirt, bruises and bug bites (as we would always forget to slather ourselves with some Off!) Ah ... those were the days.

Yes, being 5 was all about good times with friends and family. It was about playdates, bedtime stories and board games. Back then, we didn't have expensive gaming systems. We didn't watch hours and hours of television. It was a time when your mom and dad kicked you out the door first thing in the morning and told you not to come back until the streetlights came on. Those were definitely the days.

Spring

By Terry Persun

MY FAMILY DIDN'T HAVE INDOOR PLUMBING until I was 8 years old; I remember the day the sink, tub and toilet were delivered to our house. We lived on a macadam road 2 miles off Route 15 in Cogan Station, Pa. At the time, there were only a few houses on that road, separated by at least a half-mile of cornfields on either end.

Dad unboxed all of the white porcelain and set it out in the front yard until he was ready to install it. Those bathroom fixtures sat there for over a week, and all my friends who rode by with their parents could see what had just arrived at our house. I don't want to imagine what they talked about all the way to town. But when I was 5, there were much worse things than a bit of embarrassment to be concerned about.

My dad built our house with his own hands, everything from the cement block foundation to the tarpaper roof. In fact, he built three houses on that same property. I never lived in the first house but have memories of life in the second and third. The second one, which was built on stilts, almost fell over when the floods came. The third house is the one I remember growing up in. As long as I can remember, our place was always in the process of being finished. The siding covered all but the back porch for years, and the front porch didn't get closed in until after I grew up and moved away.

When I was 5, the inside of the house consisted of the kitchen (where the potbelly stove ran nonstop all winter long) and a bedroom (which also served as the living room until the other bedrooms could be finished). There was a curtain across an opening along the back wall that led to the unfinished bedrooms. We weren't allowed to go past that curtain or we would fall 7 feet into the basement. There were only studs along the floor line and studs where bedroom walls were going to be. I had many nightmares about falling into that space.

I only remember one bed in the combination bedroom-living room, but there must have been more as there were six of us by then. The family consisted of Mom, Dad and Howard (my older brother), me, my younger sister and my younger brother. The house was packed.

There was one electrical outlet in the kitchen where we plugged in the radio and the refrigerator. We had a stove that ran off propane. I remember having to do most of my business in a bucket that sat in the closet-size room that would eventually become our bathroom. My other option was to walk to the outhouse that had been erected 100 feet or so beyond the back porch. A flashlight was kept by the back door for late-night treks, but I never needed it. I only used the outhouse during the day; at other times I used the bucket.

But that's not what this story is about, and I've been avoiding the truth all this time. What I miss about being 5 years old is how close we all were — though my parents may not have felt that way. I can only imagine, now that I'm older, but to a little boy, having your whole family around was nice. There were evenings when we played cards by candlelight. We played word games and guess-what-number games. We read — sometimes alone and sometimes out loud. There was almost always paper around to write or draw on, and we were never short of crayons or pencils. What better thing for a writer?

I started school when I was 5. Maybe my parents were trying to get rid of me, or maybe it was just time — but I couldn't wait. Howard had taught me math that he learned in school. He exposed me to poetry and taught me how to read. By the time I went to school, I was excited to be there. I wanted to learn.

But there is a story behind my entering school. As my mom tells it, when I was 3 and 4, Howard would take me to school with him on special occasions — like holiday parties and bring-a-sibling-to-school day. Since I only got to go to school during the fun times, I apparently thought it was all fun and games.

Later on, I had to meet with some of the teachers before I could be admitted to attend school. The story goes that when I was asked about where an elephant's trunk was, I gave the sarcastic answer that it was in the rear, like the trunk of a car. When asked about my colors, I mixed them all up.

But I wasn't scolded like one would expect. Instead, my parents must have known what was going on, and they explained that the teacher wasn't joking. I immediately wanted to know why the questions were so easy if they weren't joking. If they really wanted to know how much I knew, I wondered, why didn't they ask me to do some addition or recite a poem? It was explained to me that they started out with the easy questions.

To this day, my mom reminds me how much trouble it was for her and Dad to convince the school to test me again. When the school finally agreed, I passed just fine. But they put me into the class with the lower students. I loved it. Those were my kind of kids: rambunctious, loud and playful. I made some important friends in that class, but I didn't stay there long. Once the teacher found out that I could not only add and subtract but also read and do some of my multiplication tables, I was put into a different class. I only saw my old friends during recess, but I eventually found other friends, too.

As the story goes, by the time I finished first grade my parents were contacted about the possibility of my skipping second grade. The teachers agreed that I was bored with my classwork, and they feared that I would stop studying or stop doing my homework — which was never going to happen with my parents. It wasn't until after the decision was made that Mom and Dad told me about the situation. They decided that I was already the youngest child in the room, and they didn't want it to become even more difficult for me to socialize. So, I moved forward one grade at a time, just like all my friends. (That progression is a whole other story.)

There was a lot going on when I was 5. Much of it was over my head at the time, but I would never give up my childhood or trade it for anyone else's. Even growing up poor, I felt as though I was a unique person and was encouraged to continue to be so. What could be better than that?

By Laura Tiberio

THE WALLPAPER, WHICH IS BLACK VELVET and gold foil, looks almost the same upside down as right side up. Standing on my head in the hallway early on a Saturday morning, I wait for the ticking clock to tell the start of my favorite cartoons. The long day is spread out before me; I have no worries, no responsibilities. Cheerios are for school days, so today it will be pancakes — warm and fluffy, with Mrs. Butterworth's famous syrup.

A friend is coming over; for two whole hours we will play! The fir tree in the backyard is our house, with rocks making the fire pit, ivy covering the beds and fragrant mock orange branches arching over our heads. In the swing, we soar higher and higher. Can we reach the boughs of the cedar with our feet? Who can touch first? Our heads thrown back, we laugh as we pump fiercely toward the clouds.

Hum, hum, creak! The garage door opens. I hear the sound of his key in the side door. The hinges squeak. The keys clank on the kitchen table. Daddy's home! I run into the kitchen. He catches me in his arms and lifts me high in the air, spinning me around. Then he pulls me in close, nose to nose; he smiles and says, "Hello, sweetheart. How was your day?"

Mom is out tonight. Daddy and I drive in the silver Mustang way up north to visit *his* mommy and daddy. I sit in the front seat with my head hanging out the window. Warm wind presses against my face. I catch it, scooping with my hands and throwing it down to the floor. The trees whiz past. A forest appears next to the gray ribbon of concrete. I see bears and deer and log cabins. I imagine running, fast as a deer, alongside the car through those lush greens. The wind brings water to my eyes, but I am not crying. I am too happy. I know we will have rigatoni and that soft buttery bread. There will be TV and popcorn — maybe even ice cream. On the way home, I lie down in the backseat covered with an old crocheted blanket — the one with the zigzag patterns in so many blues. Watching the streetlights flash by, I pass into bleary half-sleep that lasts until we get home. Then I squeeze my eyes tight so my dad will carry me into the house and right to my own bed.

The school bell rings. My grandparents are waiting. The long brown car with the creamy vinyl hood is in the exact same place every day. I crawl in between them to my spot, right in front of the radio whose dials and switches are mine to touch. We play air traffic controller all the way home. We eat canned cling peaches with vanilla ice cream. Grandpa takes me up, up, up in the elevator. He loads the clothes; I put in the quarters. Slide the metal tray back and pull it out again. Quarters are gone! It's my own magic trick.

Riding in the backseat, I watch the rain coming down. Pit, pat, splash. Outside the window, everything blurs. The tag in my coat scratches at the back of my neck. But I am smiling. We are going to the movies! After parking the shiny black car a block away, Mom pops the umbrella. Together we huddle and scurry toward the neon marquee. Seated inside the magnificent theatre, Mom turns to warn me: "Now there is going to be a dragon..." I am not worried. The curtains open; the music rings in my ears. I am joyfully lost in the dancing colors.

A fresh and sweet smell fills the house. Daddy has wrestled a tree into the red and green metal stand. Mommy has filled the bowl with water. The lights are flashing, first the blue, then the green and finally the yellow. On top of the tree, the angel blinks fastest of all. I hang the ornaments. Well, I get to do some of them — not the glass ones, of course. The stockings go over the fireplace. I seek out the little places in the rock mantel to hang them. The little house with the rocking chair in it sits on the coffee table next to the musical boy and girl. I twist the boy around; he spins and spins. I try again. I want him to stop right in front of the girl so it looks like they are kissing. The presents appear a few at a time. I wrap a can of tuna to give the cat.

One morning I awake early, and world outside is white. Boot prints cover the deck. A snow turtle peers through the railing as I slide down the hill on a plastic garbage-can lid. Hot chocolate warms my chilled cheeks as my mittens melt in a puddle on the apple-green linoleum floor. Candles flicker on the dining table, on the coffee table and on the end table. The lights are out. Warm arms snuggle me on the couch by the fire. I float on peaceful stillness to the land of dreams.

Spring

By Laura Zera

FOUR WAS KIND OF FUZZY, and 6 was stressful — reading, writing *and* arithmetic? Are you kidding me? But 5 was nothing short of fabulous.

At age 5, I got my first record album, the very hip Tony Orlando & Dawn; I played it incessantly. My mum caved in and bought me my first pet: a hamster that I named Napoleon. A week later, the hamster had babies. (And then ate them. That part, I didn't like so much).

Kindergarten included the brilliant concept of naptime, and Mrs. Sellers was the most even-tempered teacher ever. And with only a half-day of school, I still had time to watch *The Price is Right* and climb the giant cedar tree in the backyard.

Although my childhood home is gone, a recent check on Google Maps revealed the cedar tree is still there. I have half a mind to go back, reclaim my favorite perch — I'm positive those branches will still hold me — and risk being arrested for trespassing. That's what being 5 was all about: climbing high without giving a second thought to falling down. I used to be so fearless. As an adult, I've come to accept that facing fear is just one of those normal things that I need to do — sometimes on a daily basis — but I sure enjoyed the early liberty of my young spirit.

I also used to be shameless, especially regarding what came out of my mouth. When I wanted Marnie and Jessica — the two 6-year-olds who lived nearby — to include me in their cool, older-girl circle, I had no difficulty in capturing their attention.

"I have a monkey," I said. They pressed in closer as we leaned up against the chain-link fence in the schoolyard.

"Where?" Marnie asked.

"He lives in my basement. His name is Cheetah." My pause was imperceptible. "Cheetah, the monkey."

Soon enough, they were at my back door. "We want to see him," Jessica said.

I hadn't thought that far ahead, but with a quick toss of my hair, I said, "He's sleeping right now. We can't wake him up. You'll have to come back another time."

This went on for several days. Cheetah was always sleeping, eating or bathing, and these activities could not be infringed upon by a gaggle of curious girls, I told them in a most impervious tone. They clearly did not know how to rear a monkey; I most certainly did. At least I talked as though I knew. Finally, Jessica announced they didn't believe me anymore.

"Prove it," Jessica said. She and Marnie stood shoulder to shoulder with their arms crossed.

Blink. Blink, blink. "Okay, I don't have a monkey in the basement." No big deal. "Want to go play Barbies?"

It was such delicious freedom to be able to say whatever I wanted — and with great swagger and conviction. There was no filter, no concern over what people would think of me and, as I recall, no consequences for my lying until I hit age 6. (That's when I had to apologize to Marnie's dad for fibbing about picking the perennials in their garden). And while it is probably a good thing the lying and stealing have since abated, I really miss the uncensored dialogue. Back then, even if you massively screwed up, it seemed much easier to get to the point of forgive and forget.

When I was 5 years old, I was still my mother's baby, and she protected me as such. Because I was a bit afraid of things that went bump in the night, she would cuddle with me on our white Naugahyde sofa or lie down beside me in bed until I was ready to fall asleep. She would put her slender arms around me and make a funny rumbling noise (half revving car engine, half Kitchen Aid blender) as she wiggled me in closer. She never gave me just one kiss; it was always three or four.

My life changed dramatically in the years that followed. Mum had an undiagnosed mental illness, and it exacted a great toll. Eventually, I ended my relationship with her. Seventeen long years went by. I wondered time and again if there would ever be an opportunity for reconciliation.

Spring

Finally, in 2009, I learned that she was in the hospital. Dementia had set in, finding the cracks and gaps in her brain that mental illness had not yet occupied. A social worker arranged for us to reunite once Mum was settled in her new surroundings at a care home.

The first visit was easier than I expected, because my mum didn't remember me. There weren't any tense, emotionally charged moments. She was frail and addled, and easily redirected away from conversation about our past. We talked about the weather, the food in the dining room and how she liked one type of sweater over another.

On my second visit, I found my mother in her room. "Hi, Mum!"

"Mum?" Her brow furrowed. "Are you my daughter?"

"Yup, I'm Laura, your younger daughter."

As I dropped into a chair, she looked at me, and a little smile crossed her lips. "You're Laura," she said. Then, "You're Laura. You used to curl up at my feet like a kitten."

For an instant, she held a memory. Then her eyes became unfocused again, and it was gone. I held the memory, too, and then carefully filed it away in a place where I could easily retrieve it. It was a souvenir of the safe, secure days of my childhood.

When I was 5, I was fearless and shameless — except when I wasn't. And then, I was tucked in close to my mum. It was the best place in the world to be.

By Tracey M. Hansen, Co-Author

I MISS BEING NAÏVE AND UNAWARE, able to charm my way out of anything and not yet knowing what it meant to be embarrassed.

The cookies with the fudge stripes are made by elves in a tree? I believed it. A fat man comes down the chimney and leaves me presents every year on December 25th? Sold. Dr. Huxtable is such a successful obstetrician that even with six kids he can afford a brownstone in Brooklyn Heights? Yeah, I was 5, and even I didn't fall for that one.

When I was 5, my grandmother had the first computer I'd ever seen. It was huge and barely fit on the tiny computer desk in the den of her house. When my sister and I would visit, Grandma would pop in one of those black floppy disks, and I would play the very first black-and-white version of the game known as Frogger. You know, the one where you make your little masochistic frog hop across the street while he tries to avoid being hit by a car? In hindsight, it was very inappropriate for a 5-year-old, but, then again, this was also a time when cribs had a good seven layers of sturdy lead paint. I guess it's all relative.

Being an inquisitive little tyke, I asked a lot of questions. What is that? What is it made of? Who makes it? Are we there yet? Why are mommy and daddy wrestling without their clothes on?

One day, I must have been particularly annoying while playing Frogger, because when I asked Grandma who invented the game, she responded with "I did." She must have given me the shortest answer possible in order to get little Tracey to shut-the-fuck-up. Well, it worked. It worked so well, in fact, that until I was 12, I believed my grandmother invented the game of Frogger. Years after Grandma died, my father overheard me bragging about her accomplishment; he finally set me straight.

"Grandma didn't invent Frogger," he told me. The game, I was informed, came with the computer.

Thanks a freakin' lot, Grandma.

She is probably reading this in heaven right now, and I know what she's thinking: "And she *still* won't shut-the-fuck-up."

Being able to charm your way into (or out of) anything is a talent only a cute 5-year-old girl can possess. I miss having that kind of power. When I was in kindergarten, I would get out of doing the assigned busy work by walking up to the teacher's desk in five- to 10-minute intervals to ask her questions about the assignment. Once the teacher answered, I would follow up with something like "Your hair is so pretty." This usually engaged the teacher in a conversation about how my hair was pretty, too, and bought me a good 10 minutes of escape from my work.

I tried this method again in college, but I am sad to report it had an entirely different outcome. When the teacher handed back my work, not only did it have the standard big fat F on top, but next to it she had written: *Call me. Love, Loretta* ... circled in a heart.

That bitch is still all up on my Facebook page.

I miss *never* being embarrassed, even when I should have been. I miss being a 5-year-old and dancing and singing my little head off for the pure joy of it, all while being blissfully ignorant of my nonexistent talent. Nowadays, I can't even think of singing karaoke without practically stroking out.

One day my grandparents (not the same ones mentioned earlier) came over to our house, and my mom asked me to put on a show for them. I went into the other room and practiced for what seemed like hours. I finally came out dressed in my best Disney princess jammies. I used the brick step of our fireplace as my stage.

"OK, let's hear it. What are you going to sing for us?" Mom asked, as my grandparents eagerly awaited my performance. "A song from Snow White? Cinderella?"

"No, Mom, just wait," I whined.

"OK, then go." She smiled as she waited to show off me and my cuteness to her parents.

I took a deep breath, and then I started, slow and soft at first.

I think we're alone now
There doesn't seem to be anyone around
I think we're alone now; the beating of our hearts is the only sound...

Then I got louder, almost screaming.

Runnin' just as fast as we can
Holdin' on to one another's hand
Tryin' to get away into the night
And then you put your arms around me
And we tumble to the ground
And then you say ... I think we're alone now

I accompanied this song with a dance that consisted of me wrapping my arms around myself and pretending to make out with a pillow while tumbling to the floor and rolling around. My mom's face was red, and even with my grandmother's limited understanding of the English language, she, too, was a color resembling a radish.

It was the first time I truly understood and appreciated the power of shock value.

I miss that.

—WTYM

Summer

What would you tell your 20-year-old self?

By Tess Hardwick, Co-Author

I CAN SEE YOU THERE IN THE BATHTUB at the apartment across from campus. Your neck is resting on a tattered towel; there's a bottle of beer, along with bubbles and self-hatred. Your eyes are closed, and tears slip from their corners into the warm water. With your fingers, you pinch excess flesh at your waist — and you hate. You curse your own existence and yearn to be someone with a flat stomach and long legs and darker skin and hair that is not the color of dirty water. At this school for the beautiful in this city of angels, you long to be someone who is noticed — not just a benign, reliable shadow.

I want to pull your hand from the warm, soapy water and hold it between my own or run a finger across your unlined forehead and beg you to listen to me. But you cannot see me. This mirror reflects only one way. I cannot give you love. I cannot give you a stern talking to. I cannot give you a glimpse into your future so that you might avoid the abyss into which you are sinking. I despair here, far away, these 20 years turned so quickly into now. There are many things I could tell you and many choices I wish you wouldn't make during the years to come.

Your childhood was like a cocoon. You found shelter in the faces of those who loved you, in the flowing waters of the river and in the stars that glittered above as you sat on a rock still warm from the evening sun. They all whispered that anything was possible and that you mattered. That is all far away now, and you are left in a deep chasm of angry professors and stacked odds and screeching sirens or that dreams can come true or that you have anything to offer. The path you chose quashed those beliefs early and swiftly. Now you are lost, aimless and drifting. You lack the surety you felt as an adolescent, when your confidence was as fixed as the rock jutting

Summer

from the river.

On bended knee, there by the tub, I would hold your baby face in my mother hands and tell you: Go to the source. There are places to find your foundation; from these places, all can be rebuilt. I'm begging now for you to hear this. The answers are in the woods, at the ocean, in a church and in music. They are found in reading the great poets, the essays of Emerson, the stories of Alice Munro and the character of Atticus Finch in *To Kill A Mockingbird*. The answers are found on the blank page where your words can be splashed and reordered into something clarifying. All of these things will help you identify yourself. What you seek cannot be found in the glittering and seductive world. It does not lie in getting the part, winning the boy or making the grade.

I would tell you to be present in every moment. Mark it in your mind and write about it so that it's cemented there to pull out, look at and learn from. Then, I would tell you of your ravishing soul, of your way of peering at it all and ordering it into something that can be understood by others. I would tell you that physical beauty matters only to the world and not to God. He cares about that which cannot be seen. He put you here for a reason. The sooner you understand that, the sooner you will have peace.

Listen now, I would tell you. Without this soul footing, in the years to come you'll make mistakes. You'll give several years away to someone who preys upon the immense emptiness inside you that begs for another human being to fill it — just so you might prove to yourself that you are worthy of love. And the other one — the man you loved and kissed in the Seattle rain outside a bar at midnight — you will bend towards him like a tulip in repose because of the deep hole inside you, and he will leave because of it. Without holding on to your footing, to this connection and source that gives you strength, you'll give away your power. For years, you will not understand that you are more than your physical presence in this world and that forces we cannot fully understand guide us and shape us. Those forces are encased in love.

If you understood this now — instead of later when you gaze into the eyes of your first child and see something more powerful than your petty wishes and desires — then I needn't warn you of the trouble to come. If you knew this, if you could hear me, it would be enough, and you would understand that it's already time to pick up your pen and begin filling notebooks with observations of yourself and everything around you. There would be ideas for characters or stories, but mostly there would be a great release of the fury and angst — and an unleashing of a vast capacity for self-love.

But you cannot hear me. You cannot heed my warning or my advice. You are in the bathtub before attending a party, hating yourself for your imperfect appearance and your asymmetrical face.

I see you there, and I forgive you. I release you, because you are young and vulnerable and lost. I no longer cringe when I see you, knowing the mistakes that hover in the future, because I know you're doing the best you can. I know it because I'm a mother now, and I can see you as our mother must have seen you then and me now. You are enough. You are the only you. You are just right.

Summer

By Gordon Bonnet

AT MY CURRENT AGE OF 51, going back to talk to my 20-year-old self seems at first glance like a good idea.
"Yo, self," I picture myself saying. "See that girl over there? The cute one with the brown hair? The one you are seriously lusting after, the one whose brother you're trying to wheedle into introducing you? Bad idea, dude. Bad news. You're looking at 16 years of nonstop neurosis, followed by a divorce, and 10 years after *that* you'll still be wondering what the hell you were thinking when you married her. And majoring in physics, buddy? Really? It hasn't hit you yet that you hate all of your physics classes? This fact hasn't, like, clued you in that maybe majoring in this subject is *not* what you should be doing? How about majoring in something you actually *enjoy*?"

I'm guessing that 20-year-old me would probably have responded to all this in much the way he typically responded to old geezers giving him advice; namely, to say, "piss off," and go back to ogling the cute girl with the brown hair. Twenty-year-old me was not known for taking suggestions if they did not encourage him to pursue (1) beer, (2) girls or (3) music.

But presuming I could somehow break through 20-year-old me's incessant focus on partying and sex, it would have been nice to sit down and have a little chat. Whether "me" would have listened to me we'll never know, but here are a few things I would have said.

First, take risks. Okay, maybe that's a silly thing to tell a person whose proudest moment in college was scaling the outside wall of the chemistry building at 1 o'clock in the morning. Twenty-year-old me was all about physical risks; emotional risks, not so much. Twenty-year-old me hated putting himself in a situation where he might be rejected, embarrassed or laughed at. As a result, he seldom took chances, put himself out there or did things that pushed the comfort envelope. An opportunity to be an exchange student in France? No, 20-year-old me couldn't do that. Apply to a college out of state? No way. Spend the summers traveling? Too risky.

55

I would, incidentally, tell 20-year-old me that the beautiful girl he wanted to ask to the high school senior prom — but chickened out on — will show up at his 20-year high school reunion and tell him that she had a life-threatening crush on him back in high school. She'll admit to always regretting not saying anything at the time. I would tell 20-year-old me that later that night, back in the hotel room, he will cry over lost chances that never come again.

Second, I would tell him that you don't win at the game of life by having someone tally up when you die how many people you have "refrained from confronting." I wouldn't tell 20-year-old me to be an asshole; heaven knows the world has enough of those. In any case, 20-year-old me was so far from that end of the spectrum that it wouldn't have made sense to him. But I would say: "You gain nothing by letting manipulative people push you around, drain your energy and take your desires away. Be willing to push back. Be willing to stand up for what you need. Be a little self-righteous about your own boundaries, for God's sake, about what makes you you. Because there are people who will take as long as you give, and they will not understand unless you say, *enough* — and maybe not even then. But you still need to say it and mean it and be willing to walk away if they will not respect the fundamental core of you."

Next, I would tell him: "Never doubt that deep down you are a good person. You're really a pretty sweet guy, all told, and you shouldn't be ashamed of the fact that you cry over Hallmark commercials. Relax, and don't worry so much about what you *should* be; what you *are* is just fine. You need some refining, that's all, and that'll happen with time — no matter what. For now, don't try to pretend you're someone different than who you are: a quirky, passionate, fun-loving musician/science nerd who likes to climb trees, play the flute and skinny dip. A guy who thinks that kissing is about the most fun thing to do in the whole wide world. Whoever told you that you should change any of those things should never have done that, and 51-year-old me is here personally to tell them to shut the hell up."

SUMMER

And lastly, I would say, "Don't fear change. It's the way of things; the world is built that way. I don't know why, and neither does anyone else, but it's a fact. People move on, grow old, die; loss is part of life. It's okay to cry till your heart breaks when it happens, but don't let a fear of loss make you afraid to connect. In the end, you'll have lost more by turning away than you would by loving wholeheartedly and then losing the object of your love to the sad fact that all things end eventually — no matter how desperately we cling to the myth that they'll last forever. Jump in, headfirst and embrace what you have. Knowing that what you have may be gone or different tomorrow, next week or next year, doesn't make it any less sweet now. It only means that you damn well better enjoy it; savor every last drop of love and beauty and pleasure you can from it.

"So, 20-year-old me, that's what I've learned. I hope it was helpful. Here's a big hug and a pat on the back. Remember what I've said — especially about the crazy brown-haired girl who is nothing but trouble. Oh, yeah, and one other thing: Dude, you *really* should consider a different hairstyle."

57

By Galit Breen

I LEAVE THE LIGHT ON for my roommate.

It glistens through our dorm room, along with the lampposts and the stars and the moon.

She stumbles in many hours later, and we see our nights for the second time, through each other's eyes.

Whispered survival secrets passed from one college student to another.

* * *

The girls and I walk home barefoot.

Our makeup is smudged, and our curls are loosened, but our sparkle is just as bright as when this night began.

Thursday nights at the Cantina are always the same — cheap beer and bad music, cute boys and dancing with our eyes closed.

We link arms, slinging our strappy heels on manicured fingertips.

* * *

I plant my feet within the perfectly green quad.

My sunglasses on, my hair pony-tailed, my flip-flop tan crisp.

Nearby, tall boys play hacky sack and blonde girls watch.

Faint jazz filters from behind closed doors; the smell of freshly baked bread does the same.

I sit alone sketching or reading or catching up on last week's homework.

* * *

When I dig into my 20s, small vignettes — people and words and embraces and tears — puzzle piece to each other and form my memories.

Each inch-by-inch frame slightly overlaps the other, writing my story and telling my tale.

Summer

I want to look back and give myself sage advice, clear my path, smooth my edges.

Don't kiss that boy! Travel farther! And good lord — drop that class!

But that boy? Was a really good kisser.

And that trip? Ended on the sweetest note.

And that class? Ignited a passion deep within.

So I'm going to let my 20-year-old self be: barefoot walks and tear-stained cheeks and whispered secrets and all.

I like the way I've unfolded. Each puzzle piece is dependent on the next — fuzzy and blurry and confusing alone but my story when edged together.

By F. Jo Bruce

"MESELF," I GREETED MY YOUNGER SELF, "come on in. I've been wanting to talk with you for a long time."

She replied, "What do you want to tell me?"

A bright gleam from the wide, gold wedding band made me remember so well the day it was placed there. "You are so young to be married," I noted. "Meself, I will talk to you openly, honestly and very frankly. I, for one, wish you had never gotten married so young!" I said emphatically.

Her bright smile faded, a serious look replacing it. "Why?" she inquired, rather plaintively.

The door to the talk was opened. Looking into her future, I continued.

* * *

Child — and you are a child — you have your whole life ahead of you. Opportunities will come that you can't even believe exist. You should be able to become anything you want, do all the things you want, have all the fun you want and travel to all the places you want to go. Marriage is not a bad thing, certainly, but you are much too young to have embarked upon it now.

Choosing not to go to college was good for you, as you wanted to work and be out from under the routine and restrictions of school. You always hated routine (still do). If you had continued to live at home with Mom and Dad while working and thinking things through, you might have decided to further your education. I always knew your love for words and writing would grow within you. You had such an ability, even so young, to use your creative imagination to put words, ideas and dreams to use in living an independent lifestyle — free from the routine you abhorred.

You married into a good, stable family and learned much from their way of living for the 16 years you were there. That lifestyle was not your destiny ... or didn't have to be. By marrying so young, you conformed yourself.

You are an entertaining and funny person, both in word and deed. You amuse everyone you meet with your talk, actions and sense of humor. I was always flattered at the times you were told you should be on stage, as your talents were phenomenal. You could shape yourself to words and actions, become another person. You gathered children to tell them stories, spewing out words effortlessly, without thought of what you would say — and they loved it. Oh, goodness, the tales you told could have gone onto paper and into a book to be sold, making you a rich and meaningful living. Your creativity had no end.

It's a waste to live in the moment. Goodness, girl, if I had a nickel for all those moments I wasted, we both could be living in the lap of luxury.

We both giggled.

I know, from your expression, it's very hard for you to capitalize on all this wisdom I have achieved since I was your age. You will only understand when you have lived these days, months, years, as I have.

I took her small, soft hand and held it with my own.

Those hands will clean, cook, hold your baby, slap your husband in anger, cover your eyes when tears flow, nurse your mother, caress the true love of your life when he comes along and make many other reactive movements through the years. There's no way I can make you understand or even remotely believe what is ahead of you in this life. It's not all bad, but one decision you have already made — and others will take you down paths you really don't want to trod. When we grow older, we will look back and say "if only." But when we are your age, we just say, "They don't know what they are talking about."

Eyes wide, mouth open, she didn't believe a word I had said. How could I explain, convince her that I had already lived those days, months, years?

When we are young, life is a game. I played at being in love, ready for marriage. I played at knowing everything and making wise decisions. I heard what my parents said, but I didn't heed them. Not that they were always right, but they often gave me food for thought — food that I didn't partake of until I got older. By then, I was too old to go back and do some of that living again. Youth, it is said, is wasted on the young. I didn't think so when I was young, but now I know so.

We were coming to the really hard part. Soon she would go, and I had to try and get it all in, make my words count.

Meself, I developed a motto when I reached my very mature years: Never go backward, only forward; and I will go forward every day. Does that make sense to you?

She questioned me then ... wondering what this all meant. Was I telling her that what's been done cannot be undone ... but that each day is new — and you can make that day better?

Yes, that's it.

My heart lurched. I was standing before myself, not a blemish on my face, eyes bright and clear, dark hair shining, my face full of hope and youthful beauty. I gazed into her green eyes. From the look on her face, I could tell that she understood.

Remember, always go forward, trod carefully and think deeply. Use your intelligence, skills, natural abilities and talents. Avoid laziness and procrastination. Educate yourself at every turn.

Formal education is good, but nothing compares to logic, reasoning and common sense. Without those three attributes, you can't function. That's my experience and belief, and I haven't been convinced otherwise. I am old and you are young; I have told you all I know to tell you.

* * *

Our conversation had ended, and Meself retreated into the haze of years gone by. My reverie ended, I realized that I spoke not to the younger me but to my self-proclaimed wiser self — the one with the silver frost on the once jet-black hair.

Realizing that Meself and I are one, now I am listening.

SUMMER

By Derek Flynn

WHAT WOULD I TELL MY 20-YEAR-OLD SELF?
I'm not one for looking back. Don't get me wrong, I love to reminisce about the past, look at old photos, etc., but when it comes to things like "What would you tell your younger self?" I balk. I think it's too easy to get lost down a blind alley of regrets and "couldas, wouldas, shouldas." It can be debilitating and stop you in your tracks. I prefer forward motion.

But I couldn't get that question out of my head. "What would you tell your 20-year-old self?" I ran through all the different things in my head that I could possibly tell my younger self. And then, I realized something: It doesn't matter. My 20-year-old self wouldn't have listened anyway.

We hear all these clichés such as "Youth is wasted on the young" and "You can't put an old head on young shoulders." But why would you? Youth is the time when you need to experiment, to mess up, to make mistakes. (Within reason, of course. If my 20-year-old self had ended up in hospital after jumping drunk from a third-story window, I would probably tell him to stay in and watch TV that particular night!)

And there's something else that I don't think my 20-year-old self would have understood. It's something you learn as you get older and as you "create" more and more. You begin to understand that the act of creation is an end in itself, something I don't think my 20-year-old self would have been able to grasp. He wanted to be Bruce Springsteen or Bono, standing on a stage with 80,000 people in the palm of his hand. Or Norman Mailer writing the Great American Novel. (Given that I was not — and am still not — American, you can see how lofty my 20-year-old self's goals were!)

But what if all the writing was never published, all the music never listened to? Would it have been a waste of time? Of course not.

63

Then, why do it? The short answer is: It's not *just* about publication or recognition. Take someone like Kafka. He left behind a body of work that he wanted destroyed. Why? Did he not think it was good enough? When he wrote it, did he not do so with an eye to publication? Did he just write purely for the act of writing? While we all yearn for publication and recognition, at the end of the day, you're simply inspired to write.

As a kid, I was always writing: stories, comics, novels that ran the length of a 120-page copybook. Then I discovered songwriting. From the age of about 15 or 16 to around 25, that's all I did. And how much of that songwriting and novel writing was done with an eye to publication or to people hearing the music? With the songs, I just wanted to write songs — and then write better songs. And I wanted to say something, to wrestle with whatever was going on in my head. I think that's true of the novels as well.

So, what is it that the artist is trying to do with these acts of creation? What do they set out to achieve? They do it so that they can impart some gift, some manner of knowledge to people. But this doesn't make the poet a prophet; it makes them a philosopher. It makes them someone who works out issues in their art, not someone who makes pronouncements as if they know the answers to everything. Someone who works things out through their art and feels that the conclusions they draw (despite the fact that they might be incomplete or flawed) are worth sharing with the world — not as pronouncements but as suggestions. Suggestions of truths rather than absolute truths.

So, back to my 20-year-old self. As I said, I don't think he was mature enough yet to understand all that I've just said. He was cocky, insecure and probably simultaneously convinced that he was both a waste of space and the world's next big thing. That's how 20-year-olds are. Telling him that by the time he was my current age he still wouldn't be a world-famous rock star or a great American novelist wouldn't have helped. And telling him things that he might do differently to try to remedy this situation would be even worse. Ya throw the dice, ya make your choices.

Summer

Besides, as I said, he probably wouldn't have listened. I don't think my 20-year-old self could have imagined reaching my age, let alone read a long tract of do's and don'ts from me. But he — like me — was fond of aphorisms, those short, concise gems of wisdom. (My 20-year-old self and I have also always had a soft spot for Hemingway's shortest short story: "For sale. Baby shoes. Never worn.")

So, in that spirit, I will pass on an aphorism borrowed from Neil Gaiman, who, in turn, borrowed it from Clive Barker: "Never apologize. Never explain." This piece of advice was given in the context of writing, but I think it equally applies to life. And when I use that phrase, I don't mean never apologize or explain if you've done something wrong. I mean never apologize to people for being who you are. Never feel that you have to explain yourself just because others don't understand why it is you want to do what you want to do.

So, 20-year-old self, one piece of advice: Never apologize, never explain.

By Jesse James Freeman

"**IF YOU WISH TO UNDERSTAND YOURSELF,** you must succeed in doing so in the midst of all kinds of confusions and upsets. Don't make the mistake of sitting dead in the old ashes of a withered tree."
~ Emyo

It's difficult to have a dialogue with my younger self, looking so far down the road — excuse me — the roller-coaster of my life. The words must be selected carefully, and the argument must be very tight, because when I was 20, I knew everything. If you didn't believe me then, all you had to do was ask.

You didn't even have to ask nicely.

I was on a grand adventure back then, but I had no idea what my mission was exactly. That didn't matter to me, though; as long as I was moving ahead at full steam, it didn't matter where I was headed. I was still learning to communicate with people and how to interact with other humans (though I'm still not sure that I've completely figured any of that out yet).

Here's the first thing I would tell 20-Me: *The people you think are going to be the most important in your life and are going to be with you forever probably won't be hanging out for the whole ride. That's okay, though, because they don't know where their path is going to lead them either. Most of the time falling out of touch and moving on isn't anything personal, so don't take it that way.*

Next, I'd pour a drink for 20-Me and Old-Me and let the revelation set in, because there's a lot of serious ground to cover. We'd have to talk about *her* next. There aren't that many "hers" to talk about, but each one of them matters and is completely important in her own way.

She doesn't really love you. That isn't meant to be as cold as it sounds, and it's not a reflection on either of you. You're both young, and at age 20, neither of you knows as much as you think you do about the world.

Twenty-Me would argue, because that's what you do when you think you're in love. Old-Me would assure him there's no reason for that and no reason to stop believing in love in the now. It's only something that he needs to hear so he can put it all in perspective later. *It's not your fault, and it's definitely not hers. It's just what happens. Everyone goes through it; it's part of what makes us human.*

Spend as much time as you can with your family, especially your old man. No matter what the disagreement or how mad either of you may get, none of it is important. Every problem, at its best, is a temporary distraction; at its worst, it is a waste of precious time.

Never give up on the story. You are going to think you want to be a lot of different things at different stages of your life. Some of these things you will choose, most of them will be chosen for you. You're not going to have much say in how you make money; don't let this distract you. Money is nothing more than energy. Jobs, while mostly a waste of good energy, are going to be necessary for research and doing stuff like paying the rent.

There's going to be a strong argument made by those you're hanging around with at certain points in your life that you need to relax when you're not at work, that you should barbecue and throw an impromptu party every night of the week to have a little fun and blow off some steam. I'm not going to tell you, 20-year-old me, to not do this. You won't listen, and I wouldn't want to have missed out on those parties — because they were good ones.

I would tell him that if he's going to waste the time and money and all that barbecue sauce, that he should be totally in with it. There's nothing more depressing than throwing a party and not being there in spirit. It's almost as depressing as knowing you should be writing a novel 10 years before you start and then being too distracted and overwhelmed by your own baggage to do the job. But 20-Me was a psychology major, so he might catch on to that trick.

All of this sage advice, I'm thinking, might be just a waste of time for 20-Me. More to the point, it might even be a disservice. How can I be sure that I would have advice worth giving now if I hadn't made all the really stupid mistakes I made so many years ago? What if we're not supposed to listen to anyone, and it's a good thing there's no way-back machine?

I have screwed up a lot of stuff in my day, and I'm not saying this out of ego, but I'm a relatively intelligent guy. I don't think I'd be as smart today if I hadn't gone through the wrong doors more than a couple times. What sort of people can we hope to be in the end if someone never lets go of our hand and allows us to run wild?

Thanks for sharing a drink, 20-Me. Don't pay much attention to the advice I've attempted to give. Be wild, run free — and buy extra barbecue sauce.

Summer

By Laura Kilmartin

IF I HAD TO TELL MY 20-YEAR-OLD SELF just one thing, I would tell her to take more risks and not be afraid to make mistakes. It sounds incredibly trite and like every bad graduation speech I have ever heard, but it's the truth — and something I wish I had learned much earlier in life.

Often, clichés are clichés for a reason.

When I was 20, my emotional life charted like an out-of-control EKG. I was forever on the cusp of eternal happiness or the brink of disaster; there were very few moments lived in between. When a cute boy smiled at me, I had our china pattern picked out before I even learned his name. A bad grade on a paper convinced me I would flunk out of college, my family would disown me and I'd end up living in a box under a highway overpass.

As a matter of fact, I spent an inordinate portion of my 20s believing that life was one big game of *Let's Make a Deal*. Every decision — big and small — came with the possibility that I would choose the wrong door and land in that box, begging strangers for spare change. I lived a cautious youth, and the last thing I wanted to hear was that I should take more risks.

But I should have.

I should have played hooky more often. I should have spoken my mind rather than swallow my thoughts and go along with the crowd. I should have reached for things I thought were outside my grasp. I should have asked out more boys.

Convinced that taking risks was a gender-specific role cast exclusively for men, I never asked out a boy in my 20s. If a man didn't care enough to sweep me off my feet with a wild, romantic gesture, then obviously he must be repelled by my hideousness. It was love or repulsion; there was no middle ground.

I would love to tell my 20-year-old self to cut the drama. I want to tell her that she will end up asking out boys by the time she hits her 30s anyway, so she might like a little practice. I want her to know that sometimes men are thrilled to be asked — rather than relied upon to do the asking. Just like women, men need to know they are attractive and interesting.

Sometimes, when a man is asked out on a date, he will say yes and a good time will be had by all. Other times, though, a man will decline. He will give a polite "no thanks" and walk away. My 20-year-old self needs to know that while these kicks to the ego are swift and intensely painful, they are miraculously short lived. I have never witnessed a man stand up and berate a woman for daring to believe she was worthy of his time. A man refusing a date with a woman will not mock and ridicule her, leaving her a sobbing mess humiliated before a crowd of hundreds who point and chant like the extras at Carrie's prom.

I think the message I would most like to share with my younger self is this: Whatever she is afraid of, whatever worst-case scenario she has worked out in her head, I want her to know that life will never be quite that dire. I would tell her that eventually she will learn to take risks and — for the most part — those decisions will turn out pretty well. Sometimes they won't. But even the risks that don't quite work out the way she wants will not end as badly as she fears.

I want that girl to skip more classes and tell those dear to her that she loves them. Often. I wish she would argue with her literature professor and explain that — despite his opinion to the contrary — not liking *Catcher in the Rye* does not make her a sociopath.

That 20-year-old girl should try out for another play. She should not drop out of the drama club after being rejected at one audition. I wish she would take a fashion risk and wear something that makes her feel beautiful — rather than the uniform leggings and tunic top deemed stylish in the day. And she really should make a move on that guy in her philosophy class.

I would tell my 20-year-old self to put her name on the anonymous poetry she submits to the school newspaper. No, the poems aren't very good. They are overbearingly earnest, filled with

SUMMER

stale metaphors and have a weak rhythm. But they are her words, and someday she will regret having orphaned them.

Finally, I would tell that 20-year-old that she will lose far more sleep in her lifetime thinking about things she should have done than thinking about things she wishes she hadn't. That thought alone is worth some risks.

Write for the Fight

By Marni Mann

EVERY BREATH YOU TAKE isn't a made-for-reality-TV moment. Breathe slowly, enjoy every second and exhale even slower to savor it. Appreciate life as it happens. Don't rush or dwell on the trivial. Dark days are ahead; they're like nothing you've ever experienced or felt, and they're going to drain the air from your lungs.

You're going to question your path and purpose, wonder why you can't get your footing, and ask yourself, "Why me?" College is preparing you for those times. It's teaching you how to prioritize and multitask. It's showing you how to strike a match when the light goes out.

You're constantly inspired; you just haven't found the right outlet. You've taken writing for a test drive — and you enjoy it. Now you need to unleash the creativity that pulses in your veins, apply passion and emotions to your words, and allow each story to take on a life of its own. In about seven years, you're going to start writing your first novel. The topic will be addiction. Take a look around you right now; future characters, stories, plot twists and experiences surround you. You need to absorb and remember every detail, because your novel is unfolding right in front of you. In the meantime, clock some experience. Write for the university newspaper, pay more attention during your English classes, and learn the difference between a comma and a semicolon.

Because you're young, you're stumbling over yourself and preventing your own ascendancy. Love yourself. Smile more. Be proud of who you are. You were given one body and one mind, so you need to take care of them and treat them with respect. Don't hide behind your shadow because you fear judgment or wandering eyes. Self-confidence exists within you, but you need to find its root and water it so that it reaches its utmost depth and highest height.

You're afraid of getting hurt. Doubt and indecisiveness linger in your subconscious. You've witnessed the difference between moral and immoral, and you know the results of both. To protect yourself, you thicken your skin by adding layers. You believe the right person will break through those layers, unveiling the love that's hidden beneath. But you're forgetting they won't be armed with an ax. Give them a chance to meet the real you, sample your voice and appreciate what you have to offer. You don't have to strip your skin, just thin out your armor.

Listen to your elders. That includes your parents, professors, friends of friends and anyone willing to speak to you and give you advice. You believe they're giving you attention because it's their duty and obligation as an adult, and you think every conversation is a covert lecture. Don't let their words go to waste; they know what they're talking about. Absorb, process and apply. You never know when something they say will click two of your puzzle pieces into place, answer something you have been pondering or create an opportunity that otherwise wouldn't be available.

When you close your eyes at night and your mind is full of images and aspirations, hold on to those dreams. Your future is not yet written. Don't let anyone tell you, "No." Any goal is attainable, but it takes time and hard work. You have it in you. Failing is part of the equation to success. So, when you fail — and you will — learn from those mistakes and try again. Feeling afraid and being a coward are not the same thing. Fear is a way of showing caution, and no one will fault you for moving at a slow pace. They will be disappointed, though, when they know your potential and find that you are standing still.

You think you're invincible, that disease is a myth, and that your friends and family are healthy and will live forever. Death is going to hit you hard. You're going to lose people you love, and you won't always get a chance to say goodbye. Don't stop communicating. Make every goodbye count. Everyone in your life is there for a reason, but you won't realize their importance until they're gone. The words, "I wish," are said too often. Reality always stings, but it's easier to heal when remorse isn't part of the pain. There's no such thing as not enough time. Make time.

You're going to tell people later in life that you don't have any regrets — that everything you did or didn't do was a lesson. It's a lie. There are things you're going to regret. Go ahead and do, experience and accomplish, but don't hesitate. Use your brain and not your heart when you make decisions. You think you are allergic to change, that it will make you break out in questions, fear and failure. It won't. Embrace change. And don't be afraid of taking risks. Your future is going to be full of attempts and unknown results, and each one will make you stronger. Hang in there, kid. The best is yet to come.

By Karla J. Nellenbach

DEAR KARLA/KARLIE CIRCA 1999,

I hope this letter finds you in good health. If I remember correctly (Hey, I'm old, and you know how they say the mind is the first thing to go? Well, they were right. Limey bastards!), this is the beginning of the year. You're fit and spry now, but at the end of it ... well, not so much. But never fear! You will live, er, minus your appendix ... and your tonsils ... and those little gland things at the back of your nose. But you don't need that shit anyways, so it's all good.

Wow. That was a ramble and a half. Note to self: As you get older, you tend to go off on tangents. This is not always a bad thing and can lead you to many an epiphany while writing. Embrace the ramble.

Anywho, as I was saying. Now, that I've lived a good many years, I've learned a few things along the way — little bits of wisdom that I feel should be imparted. Hopefully, they will help you on your way to this ripe old age that you are currently enjoying.

1. Whatever you do, DO NOT allow Amy to cut your hair in a "cute style that is so you." I don't care how many times she says to just trust her. You will end up looking like a lesbian lumberjack version of Chris Farley ... on crack. NOT PRETTY!

2. Keep your distance from Ralph on New Year's Eve 2002. He may be lots of fun before and for about an hour after midnight, but afterward ... well, his name describes him fairly well. He will ruin not only your dress but those cute blue shoes that cost a fortune (which you'll be paying for on your credit card for six months).

3. Trust your gaydar. This is the year when you meet a great guy, one that you immediately think is a rainbow-flag-waving friend of Dorothy. When you casually drop the question of his sexuality in conversation, he will deny his gayness. Your gut will know the lie for what it is, so trust it. Otherwise, you will waste a good three months of your life dating a boy who secretly likes boys.

4. At this point in your life, your dad is not in the best of health. There will be many, many, many times in the years to come where you worry that he won't be around much longer. His good health — or lack thereof — will lead you to make decisions that you normally wouldn't have. Rest assured; Dad will make it through some scary times. (Mom and I agree that he has an angel permanently welded to his shoulder and will outlive us all.) Never forget how important family truly is, even though sometimes you want to strangle your mother. (Christmas of 2004 being a prime example.)

5. This year, you will go through a phase where you try all the illegal things you should've been doing back in high school with everyone else but were too "focused and serious" to partake in. I'm not going to go all adult and after-school special on you and tell you not to have fun, but I will say this: June 23, 1999, is so not the night to conduct any such experiments. You will freak out, BIG TIME, beginning with throwing your brother's air freshener out the window into oncoming traffic (because it turned into a king cobra and started speaking to you). Then you will pick every single topping off the pizza your friends ordered and place each olive, pepperoni slice, mushroom, etc., in their own respective piles before hurling the decimated crust into the garbage. You will shoot rubber bands at your (gay) boyfriend while calling him a fascist pig and then round out the night by sitting with your nose pressed to the TV screen watching the *Wizard of Oz*, convinced the munchkins are sending you secret encrypted messages about the upcoming apocalypse. Good times. Suffice it to say, this was not one of your better nights, and it also happened to be the last time you experimented with anything.

6. Don't lose your sense of humor. You will need it many times over the next few years — especially in the winter of 2001. Shortly after you get a much-deserved promotion at the bank, you will do the unthinkable and leave the bathroom with your skirt tucked up in the back of your pantyhose. While you are working the drive-up teller window on a very busy Friday afternoon, you will be treating many a customer to an eyeful of Karla for a full 10 minutes before a

helpful someone clues you in. Good thing you wore your cute underwear that day.

7. Write! You've already begun your journey toward becoming a published author by starting your first manuscript. I won't lie. The road will be long, winding and not without its bumps, but the ride will be insightful and rewarding. Keep on keeping on, and you will get there. I promise.

I'm sure there is so much more that I could tell you about what is to come, but wouldn't you much rather find out what's in store for you all by yourself? I know I would, if I were in your shoes.

Oh wait. I am in your shoes.

So this is my letter to you, Karla/Karlie. Put these little pearls of wisdom to good use on your journey, and I will catch your act on the flip side.

Love,

Karla

(Not many people call us Karlie anymore. Well, except for family. We're adults now, after all.)

Oh, and P.S.: Those "your mom" jokes you love so much right now? You haven't grown out of them yet … to your friends' great misfortune. I'm just saying.

By Terry Persun

AT AGE 20, I WAS COCKSURE AND REBELLIOUS. I hated taking orders, and I disliked being told what I was or was not capable of. I knew what I could do and was damned sure that I could prove it, too. I had joined the U.S. Air Force in January, when I was still 19. By the time I turned 20 later that year, I had gone through basic training in Texas and moved to Biloxi, Miss. At Keesler Air Force Base, I attended classes to become an Avionics Navigation Systems Specialist, Air Force Specialty Code 32851.

My wife was pregnant with our third son; our second son had died at 5 months old, and we were both still recovering from the loss. We never would overcome it completely, and that, in part, would eventually end our marriage. There were other matters that would attribute to the breakup, but they happened after my 20th year.

We lived in a trailer that was situated off base in a large trailer park with a pool built in the center of it. Eventually, we moved to a second, less expensive trailer on someone's private property. On most days, I got up at 5 a.m. and drove with a friend of mine to the base. We met with other airmen at the barracks and got into formation so that we could be marched to our classes. At the end of the day, we were marched back to the barracks.

The people in charge of marching us to and from our classes weren't any older than we were. In fact, at 20, I was older than most of them. I hated the whole hierarchy, so I fucked around a lot while marching. Because of the ornamentation that hung around their shoulder and under their arm, the kids in charge were called ropes. More than once, one of the ropes pulled me from the group to reprimand me for talking or to order me to march separately.

Once at class, I was much more interested in the activities of the day. I graduated at the top of my class, acing most of the tests because I knew more about electronics than half of my instructors. This was due to my high school shop classes and three years working for a major appliance and television repair shop. At a certain point, I figured the Air Force was just a job, and as long as I could do the job, I'd be fine.

On weekends, I would join my friend and neighbor, Errol, to drive the highways searching for discarded soda bottles. Errol had an old VW, and I drove a beat-up Ford Mustang — baby blue. His VW was much better for driving down into the gullies in the median of the highway. That Bug easily bounced over the curb or shoulder of the road, and if we got stuck, the car was light enough for us to push it out. Truth is, we only got stuck once. A few times, we drove several miles down the median strip. At the end of a few hours, we'd turn in the bottles we'd collected, collect our cash and head to the grocery store. Between soda bottle deposits and giving blood a few times a month, Errol and I were able to supplement our low military income, which was somewhere around $350 a month.

By the time I graduated, I knew I wouldn't be staying in the Air Force forever, but that didn't stop me from enjoying my time while I was there. At my next base, MacDill Air Force Base, I was assigned to the 555th Tactical Fighter Squadron, deployed from the 8th Tactical Fighter Wing. I loved working on the F-4 Phantoms at the base. As a training base, the equipment had to be spot on at all times. Our jobs meant something — preserving the lives of the pilots — and we took pride in what we did. I worked on some of the most complicated equipment and could repair any problem that arose. On swing- and mid-shifts, I enjoyed the solitude of the flight line and the workbench equally. When on call, I took the obligation seriously.

My son, Mark, was born in Florida. I used to sit on the steps of our trailer and read to him and his older brother, Terry, late at night. We didn't have a lot of money or time, but what we had held us together. My wife worked a part-time waitressing job, which meant that I often took care of the boys during the day and she took over at night. I was a writer even then, filling notebooks with thoughts, observations and stories. Rereading them now, I'm often floored by the insight of that 20-year-old — not only his ability to know himself but to make observations about the world around him.

That's when I started college, which was one of the primary reasons I had chosen to join the Air Force. I knew that without the GI Bill, I most likely would not finish college or be able to buy a house. My time in the service had been planned and calculated for almost a year before I made the decision to join. I've always thought things through and evaluated my life, even as I bucked the system.

I'm glad I've taken this time to get into that mindset again. As I recall the need to collect bottles and give blood, the enjoyment of technical work and the blessing it was to spend long hours with my sons, I can't help but wonder if my 20-year-old self might have more to say to me than I have to say to him. After all, I am reminded how unafraid I was to go at life with everything I had. I remember my cocky attitude, my intelligence and my belief that I could do anything. I think, with age, I have forgotten how to dive in with both feet, how to leap off the edge and figure out how to fly on the way down.

Truth be told, my 20-year-old self would be telling me not to worry about my age but to grab my goals with both hands, to stop letting other people tell me how I should or shouldn't act, and to write more often and with more freedom. Decades of living have taught me that time tends to make you cautious, make you not want to hurt anyone's feelings or piss anyone off. As you age, there's a notion that you get through life more easily. But that wasn't what brought me here, and although I might still be labeled "hard to work with" by some, I'm not half as free-minded as I once was. I don't take half as many risks. I think I'd be better off to forge a new attitude and become a bit more cocksure and rebellious again. I should construct a way of living that gets me into the middle of life — instead of along the edges where nothing's going on.

I'm going to listen to my 20-year-old self and address life with more gusto.

Summer

By Laura Tiberio

NO DOUBT, MANY HAVE HOPED during the course of life for the opportunity to give advice to their younger self. Looking back from the age of 37, what would I tell you, my 20-year-old self? What knowledge would I impart? What wisdom should I share? What lessons could I teach? Should I even try? Well, here goes...
Dear 20,

News flash. You will not go to medical school; instead, you will graduate, get married, buy a house and start a family. By the time you are 32, you will have three kids. You will always work but not often for money. In a single week, you will spend more hours cleaning your house than you ever imagined devoting to the task over the course of your entire lifetime. And yet, your house will perpetually look like a toy store collided with a garbage truck in the center of your living room.

Never mind. This might not be quite so inspiring — nor would it motivate me to finish college. Ok. So, what else? What other hopes for the future float around in that youthful brain? Right. Motherhood.

You know those five kids you always wanted? Well, you get three. But motherhood — as in the day-in, day-out, 18-to-25-year sentence of teaching self-care skills and molding young minds — is not exactly what you thought it would be. Your famous even temper? Watch it vanish before your eyes while struggling to shoe a 3-year-old. Your vast ocean of patience? See it drain away when your 10-year-old looks at you blankly and says, "Homework? Oh, I left that at school ... again." And your sense of accomplishment? That will blow away like so many leaves in an autumn gale as you finish sweeping the floor only to have your son tromp to the middle of the kitchen, remove his boots and — in the process — empty what seems to be the entire sandbox on the floor. And who is that woman you see before you? She looks like you and sounds like you, except

81

the words coming out of her mouth ... those are the very things you swore never in a million years to say.

Forget it. This would not be encouraging. In fact, it might be downright depressing. And I doubt I would believe it ... for until you are deep in the bowels of parenthood, you will have absolutely no point of reference for being responsible for another human being 24 hours a day, seven days a week. So, something besides that. Homeownership perhaps?

You will buy a house: a little white house on a sunny corner overlooking a rolling green park. And you will love it. You begin your family in this place, the babies arriving every three years in the spring. You will pour hours of love and sweat into making it your dream. Then you will move. You will desert the building you have spent more than a decade remodeling while living in dust, makeshift kitchens and beds tucked under the eaves. You will abandon this safe haven where your children learned to crawl, where their passing years were measured out in so many colored-pencil ticks on the basement doorjamb. Tear tracks will burn down your cheeks as you pack. You know why you looked for a new home; hauling three kids and your mother along to open houses every Sunday, staying up late poring over Web postings and searching for a miracle. And you know why you signed, despite your son's pleading, your daughters' hesitation and your own heartache.

Seriously? Would I even consider buying a house if I knew all this? Next!

Your dad will die when you are 29 and pregnant with your second child. Your family will struggle with this loss. Be aware, be conscientious, be hyperdiligent. Do whatever you can to prevent this tragedy. But could it really be prevented? Was it really your choice to make? Would knowing make you a more compassionate daughter? Could your attention, your influence have made a difference?

This one is hard. Really hard. Stay-up-late-at-night-crying-your-eyes-out hard. My gut-instinct first reaction is YES! You need to know this! You need to change the path. Help him see; help him live! Then I think: NO! This would be heartbreaking. If you knew, tried with all your might and he died anyway, how would that make you feel? How would that alter your course? Then my heart breaks all over again, and I really don't know. If I could reach back in time and share this with you, would I even have the strength?

After racking my brain, after pondering the many paths my life has taken, I am left with the realization that to offer you this wisdom or insight would instead be shattering dreams.

If I could tell my young self anything, it should not take the form of details regarding future employment, family tragedy or even winning lottery numbers, (though the latter is very enticing.) Instead, I believe the most beneficial thing to give someone with a life still stretched out before them is encouragement. So, I will try again.

Do not allow missed opportunities to darken your mind. You make good choices for your family, although they do not always (at the time) feel best for you.

Think on this: Life is an amusement park — the whole park, not just one ride. At times life is most like the rollercoaster, moving from fast and fabulous to terrifying and tearful. Other times it will seem more like a merry-go-round, spinning endlessly to the same tune as you ride the same painted horse up and down while peering out at the same landscape. There will be darts lobbed at a balloon to POP! and win your heart's desire. But some will stick with a disappointing thud in the pockmarked wall while someone else carries off your treasure. There are tunnels of love to share quiet moments of hand-holding and Ferris wheels for fantastic views and stomach-churning heights. At the house of mirrors, you will see yourself in all different shapes and sizes, as you may well appear throughout the course of your life.

Trapped. Grateful. Stressed. Thankful. Overwhelmed. Joyful. Alone. Loved. These emotions will rise and fall in you like the tides, sometimes leaving you so full that you wonder why they do not spill over you and wash you away. But you are strong. You will hold fast, even in the face of dissolution and doubt. Sometimes you will be so happy, your heart and mind bursting with love and joy, that you cannot comprehend sadness ever entering your life again. And sometimes you will slip on a puddle of your own tears and fear to drown in their waters. But know this: You will triumph. Your life will touch many people. Your spirit will survive births and deaths. Your mind will continue to dream, both the possible and the impossible. Your heart will achieve its greatest goal.

You will make a difference.

With Love,
37

Summer

By Laura Zera

THE YEAR WAS 1989. The place was Burnaby, British Columbia. I was a full-time university student at Simon Fraser, part-time cashier at Beaver Lumber (which we affectionately called The Wooden Tampon) and a 24/7 sentimental fool. Fortunately, only the last one still applies.

When I look back at my 20-year-old self, I have strong feelings of protectiveness followed by deep sighs. Given the chance to share a few insights with the young woman that I was, I would tenderly put an arm around her shoulders, and here is what I would tell her.

The physical

• Hair is not meant to defy gravity. When a certain someone in your economics class (whom you have a crush on) starts drawing stick figures of you and your vertical bangs, get a clue. Alternatively, you could try to trademark the look before Cameron Diaz famously replicates it in the future blockbuster *There's Something About Mary*.

• I applaud that you are going to use your semester break to backpack across Europe, but do you really need to pack those giant shoulder pads? And wear them under your T-shirts?

• Don't listen to people who say that your yellow '76 Mustang is from Ford's butt-ugly series of model years. The car is hot. The Care Bear on the dashboard is totally trendsetting, and when you drive around sporting red lipstick and shades with the music cranked, you are turnin' some heads. Don't be shy. Own it.

• After quite the dry spell in '88, this year will be fruitful for encounters with handsome young suitors. Most of them will materialize on the aforementioned trip to Europe, but your young lust will be largely thwarted by your dormitory accommodations. Instead, you will be more likely to fall asleep to the sound of the guy in the next bed heaving into his shoes. Step cautiously in the morning.

The spiritual

This section will be short, because you're not quite there yet. But know this: You have all the answers that you are looking for; you just need to quiet your ego and listen to your intuition. Pay very close attention to your energy and the energy around you. Learn to meditate! Most importantly, trust yourself. It will help you find your peaceful space.

The mental

- Just because you wrote that you were going to get a business degree on your Miss Burnaby pageant application three years ago (and then walked the fashion show portion wearing a suit and carrying a briefcase) doesn't mean you can't change your mind. Your calculus insomnia isn't going away. You're never going to learn to love accounting. You're never even going to understand accounting. Get out now and pick a different major. Embrace the fact that you like to learn about people, places and systems from all around the world. Nourish your global curiosity. It will shape your compassion in ways that will serve you far better than understanding derivatives.

- Your left-handed/right-brained-ness is really going to screw your chances of effectively learning a second language. Don't give up, though. You will really need it down the road with the places you are going to go!

The emotional

Phew, boy. This is the difficult part, grasshopper. I'm sorry to say, it's only going to get tougher before it gets better. *But it will get better.*

- Your mum. She loves you very much, but she's never going to be the mother that you dream about. Weird behavior, aggression, paranoia. She has schizophrenia. I'm telling you this now, because no one from the medical establishment is going to call it for another 20 years. So, try not to let it get to you when she acts out. Don't take it personally when she won't open her door to your visit. And give yourself a lot of credit for the work that you've put into trying to make the relationship work after leaving home five years ago. Unfortunately, there will be a time in the near future when you are going to have to put your own health and well-being first and choose to walk away completely. *It will be the right thing to do.* Try to enjoy whatever little bits you can with your mum now. And take photographs, because you're not going to have her in your life again for a very long time.

- Your big sister. She is your rock; don't be afraid to lean on her. She wants to be there for you. (She also wants to borrow your clothes, and, after everything she's done for you, you should smile sweetly and hand them over — even your favorite acid-wash denim shirt.)
- You. You want a life rich in family and friends, but in order to get close to the ones who matter most, you have to love yourself first. All of those mere mortals who bring on the panic attacks that make your stomach nauseous and your palms sweaty — the sweet boss who likes to mother you, that cute boy in economics class, your dad — they all love you already. You don't need to worry so much about what they think of you. They know you're not perfect, and they don't care. Your beautiful spirit and all of the goodness that you have to give to the world is visible to them. Dear one, don't take too much longer to see it for yourself.

By Tracey M. Hansen, Co-Author

WHAT WOULD I TELL MYSELF 10 years ago at age 20? That's both simple and complicated. I was unhappy with myself and embarrassingly mean to others, and I didn't have the self-confidence to realize I was worth more than I was allowing myself to accept.

Basically, I was a sad and whiney little bitch.

So here are some things I would tell my 20-year-old self:
- Grow some balls. You are letting everyone and their Aunt Tilly walk all over you. You are beautiful, smart and loved. So fucking act like it!
- GO OUT! Get to a bar or a club, talk to some strangers and make some really fun bad decisions! You're too young to be a hermit!
- Use a spray-in heat-protecting product on your hair before you flatiron it. This will save you tons of money in damage restoration in the future. And those glue-in extensions will lead to nothing but trouble.
- Don't go out on Halloween 2000. You're going to wreck your sexy little Hyundai Accent because you are too busy adjusting the angel wings of your costume to concentrate on not driving into oncoming traffic. P.S. — Your costume is super cute, but you still suck at driving.
- A few years down the road, you are going to want boobs. Go smaller. Great bras are a pain-in-the-ass to find in larger sizes. Victoria's real secret is that her inventory sucks.
- Don't be mean to people just because you are unhappy. You are in charge of your own happiness. You will live with the guilt of being a crazed meany pants for a long time. So, stop being so judgmental and rude! It's also very hard to live down the reputation of being a bitch.

Summer

- Finish college. Just because you can make good money without your degree doesn't mean that you won't look back and regret not finishing. It's only a few credits. Put the vodka down and attend a class, why don't ya?
- Buy all of the Michael Jackson memorabilia you can. Trust me on this one.
- You will meet the love of your life on MySpace when you are 24. Yes, I know this sounds like a bad Lifetime movie, but it's true. He will be the one to distract you during bumpy flights so that you don't get scared, the one who will hold your hand so that you don't walk into traffic, who will not be afraid to be silly with you, who will encourage you to pursue all of your dreams, the one who will ... well, he's just *the one*. Trust me.
- Dad has been right all these years. Your sister *is* your best friend — even though sometimes you would like to roundhouse kick her in the teeth. All those years of tormenting you when you both were kids will seem like a distant memory when, like a knight in shining armor, she will come to your rescue — no questions asked, no judgments passed — many, many times.
- Write. For the love of God, write! I'm told you have a knack for it — well, at least according to close relatives and other biased parties.
- The John Mayer concert you will attend when you are 24 is a dry concert. Bring a full flask; alcohol is an absolute necessity in order to enjoy a John Mayer concert.
- Pawn everything you own of value and buy stock in Google, Facebook and Apple.
- In a few years, you will want to buy a luxury condo. You will be dazzled by the plans for a fitness center and Olympic-size pool, as well as the manicured lawns and well-kept grounds — not to mention the spacious living area. DON'T DO IT! The condo complex will be made into low-income housing. Your condo will be broken into, the value will literally become zero in the eyes of the property appraiser, and flashing red-and-blue police lights will be a constant outside your window. The three other units on your floor will

become marijuana grow houses — which will be the only plus of the entire condo-buying debacle.

- At the age of 29, you are going to get a bug up your ass to run a half marathon. Train REALLY, REALLY hard for it, because your sister is going to video your triumphant crossing of the finish line. You want to avoid her also capturing the voice of the little boy in the background who shouts, "Look mommy, she's dead last!"
- Don't be afraid to be you. You are funny, a bit neurotic, loyal to a fault and, most importantly, good enough. Reach higher. You can and will get there. I promise.
- Oh, and your dream of becoming a published author will come true in a legitimate way, so you can go ahead and scrap your plans to sleep your way to the top.

P. S. — Watch what you eat and exercise more. That way, at age 30, I can avoid the diet I'm currently on (which rivals the eating habits of a small forest animal). Mmmmmm-k?

—WTYM

Autumn

What, at this point in your life, do you want, wish and dream of for your life going forward?

By Tess Hardwick, Co-Author

IT IS GLORIOUS AUTUMN, with gold and orange and red leaves fluttering in the crisp October breeze; sometimes these leaves hover in the air, suspended between the green bud they once were and the dry flakes they will become when they return to the earth.

I am an autumn leaf, somewhere between before and after. This is my now, with work to do and love to reap and sow before I land gently on the ground to merge with the earth as I meet the source, my Maker.

My dreams are defined now that I'm unencumbered by youthful angst and solidly grounded in my middle age. The paths traveled thus far have brought me to this exact moment, to the adventure of my middle years. My mind is solid and darting, still a sponge. I surge with the fire that comes from knowing what I want and who I am. I've let go of the nonsense, the worries over being enough.

There are dreams and ambitions beckoning in the long nights when I cannot sleep and during the light-filled days that disappear the instant they begin. Being a writer (and not a monk), I have not yet evolved from having some dreams of the material variety. I imagine a home by a creek near the mountains, coupled with days of streaming sun glinting and sparkling on snow. I dream of a vacation dwelling near the ocean, where I can feel small yet vital. In these places, I imagine, too, an office with a window to look out upon God's glorious landscape while I fill blank pages with my words, writing for my supper while affording Dave pursuit of his own dreams — as he has done for me these many years. I wish for best-seller lists and awards and respect from my peers. And this, above all: to perfect the craft of this vocation I love.

I anticipate the sensual pleasures still to come. And just like the child I once was, I remain awed by their existence: books to read and read again; movies to see; food and wine and visual art to feast upon; and music, always that, to bring me closer to the God I seek. There will be late-night talks with my children and swimming in the rivers of my childhood and in oceans with aqua water near white sand. There's a bed with downy warmth in the winter months and Dave's foot to reach for in the dark. I will travel with my girls and, later, after they are grown, with Dave to romantic cities, meadows and the sea. There I will pen what I see and learn. I will enjoy walking trips in Europe, road trips across America and a train ride over the hills and valleys of Canada — just like a character from Alice Munro's stories.

And there are lofty inner goals, those that cannot be seen but which matter more than all the rest. Among these are to laugh hard whenever I can and to weep without restraint when I'm sad. I will do the latter knowing now that the only way through pain is to feel it, to allow it to course through your veins and understand that someday it will be a teacher. I long to be the friend I've sought and found in others, to be an encourager, a light, a beacon of hope as a writer, teacher, mentor and seeker. I hope to develop insight and a clear mind to use in my work. To be more like Ralph Waldo Emerson and understand that nature is the pathway to God. To be still enough to hear His voice.

I hope to be a good mother — perfect in my imperfection — and to love my children without restraint, as this is the only gift they need from me. I desire to teach them a keen sense of staying present, of enjoying each moment, because I now know how fleeting time is. Knowing they are separate from me and will have their own paths and winding roads, I want to be loving and generous to them with my affection and time — without losing myself entirely within their dreams.

I look forward to all of this, yet I am sobered to remember that with each year my daughters become that much closer to leaving for their own lives, their own adventurous exploits. I can't imagine it now, watching them frolic before me with their imaginary games and joyous welcoming of knowledge. Everything is still magical and new to them, as it was for me as a child.

Mostly, I hope to be mindful of every moment during this transitory life, to appreciate the small and big wonders of my unique journey, to breath in this life as deeply as I can.

WRITE FOR THE FIGHT

By Gordon Bonnet

What's left to do?
Fifty-one, joints creak a bit, slowing down.
A few white hairs, but still moving, pace steady, back straight.
Still facing forward. Still moving daily into the unknown.
And on most days,
Still challenging fear, still learning.
What's left to do?
There are stories left to tell,
The voices of a thousand characters left to hear,
Plots to spin, webs to weave,
Ensnaring character and reader together.
And at night, when the computer is turned off,
The tale left unfinished,
That fearful little voice saying, "What will happen? Will they survive?
Does the hero slay the dragon?
Does he win the hand of his true love?
Will they live happily ever after?"
And honesty demands an indefinite answer:
"You'll just have to wait and see, wait till I reach the end,
Because only in writing do I find out the answer myself.
And sometimes the truth is that a happy ending only means
Pushing the shadows aside for a short time."
What's left to do?
Always music to be played,
Driving tunes to swing dancers across the floor.
Rhythmic synergy, when the music and the dance unite
The musicians and the dancers and the air,
Caught up in a spiral of sound.
There's always new music; there's always old music,
And old music made new by the love of the players.
What's left to do?

Autumn

Each year, a new batch of students to teach,
To praise, to encourage, to cajole,
To urge forward, to rein in,
To instruct and to learn from.
To show the world, and say, "Look! See how cool it is,
This place where we live? How can you not see it and be amazed?"
What's left to do?
A whole world of places to see.
The lush jungles of Costa Rica, the pristine temples of Japan,
Scuba diving on the Great Barrier Reef,
Eating Thai food ... in Phuket,
Seeing hornbills fly in South Africa,
Poling a raft up the Yangtze,
Standing in the marble ruins where Zeus once was worshipped,
Walking amongst the sandstone walls of Petra,
Climbing through the thin air to reach Machu Picchu.
What's left to do?
Friends to encourage, laugh with, cry with.
My children to watch, making their way, figuring out
Life's mysteries and sometimes learning that there are things whose reason
We don't know, can't know, may never know.
Lots of meals to be shared, pints of brown ale to be clinked together,
Walks to be taken with people whose lives have become so entwined in mine
That we cannot be separated — not if time or space or death
Were to cut those bonds.
What's left to do?
A lifetime's worth. And whatever fraction of it
Time and fortune will allow.

By Galit Breen

4 P.M. (3½ HOURS UNTIL BEDTIME)
"How about Play-Doh? A fort? Books? Puzzles? Paint? What do you want to *do*?" I ask.

"Can we watch a movie, Mama?" they answer.

My eyes are bleary. My other half is working late, and two hours of a movie and popcorn and snuggles and quiet sounds like nothing.

Perfect, blissful *nothing*.

4:15 p.m. (3 hours, 15 minutes until bedtime)
Movie in, popcorn popped, cozies donned.

4:30 p.m. (3 hours until bedtime)
"Hey!" reads the text from my friend Kate. "Do you want to take the kids ice-skating?"

Sitting! Relaxing! *Nothing!*

But ice-skating.

Magical, gliding, smooth, we've-never-been-before *ice-skating!*

4:45 p.m. (2 hours, 45 minutes until bedtime)
We gather our snow pants and snow boots and ice skates and helmets and hats and gloves and mittens and scarves and chairs and a sled for Brody to sit in, of course.

5 p.m. (2½ hours until bedtime)
I stand still, take it in.

The flooded-out field goes on for miles, a shiny, sparkling canvas for sharp, new skates and excited, ambitious skaters.

The moment fleets as I'm jolted back to the reason we're here.

"Let's go!" our kids squeal.

Their achingly independent feet run down the path, slide across the ice and untangle the mysteries of their ice skates.

"Push your feet in. Yes, like that," Kate explains. "Lace tight, even tighter. Stand tall, even taller."

Our bundled children are lined up in a neat, huddled row, each one waiting for their turn to learn how to master the ice.

And one by one, Kate teaches them.

Whispered survival secrets passed down from one native Midwesterner to another.

And then, they go. They waver and fall and bruise and try again. But most of all, they go.

They glint of winter.

Rosy cheeks, red noses, sore tushys, heartbreakingly big smiles.

6:45 p.m. (45 minutes until bedtime)

We trudge back to the car, our voices quieter, our steps heavier.

7 p.m. (a half-hour until bedtime)

The snow pants and snow boots and ice skates and helmets and hats and gloves and mittens and scarves and chairs and even the sled invade our mudroom in one shockingly sloshy pile that absolutely screams *FUN*.

7:15 p.m. (15 minutes until bedtime)

Bath bubbles, warmth, laughter and yawns (that they'd rather I not see).

7:30 p.m. (BEDTIME)

"Mama, can we watch that movie now?"

7:45 p.m. (15 minutes past bedtime)

Movie in, popcorn-for-dinner popped, cozies donned.

Sometime ... far, far beyond bedtime

I sit snuggled between so many pieces of my heart, bare to the world but bungee-corded to me.

My pieces are lost in their movie. Another world, another time, a slice of someone else's magic.

They fight their heavy eyelids, breathing in sweet, deep sighs that only children give in to.

Yes, there could have been writing and Facebook and Twitter and — my heart be still — perhaps even reading a real book tonight.

But instead, there were snuggles and magic and breathing and that big sloshy pile that can wait until tomorrow.

Tonight, I lived well, focused softly.

When I dare peek at my Life List, it is daunting. These heart-wants are woven through every fiber of my being.

I want to run and write and be successful in both.

And most of the time, I am unwavering on my path toward them.

But on this path, beneath my fibers, at my core, I hope that I have the wisdom and the grace and the know-how to do what I did today.

I hope to live well and focus softly — every day.

AUTUMN

By F. Jo Bruce

AT MY BABY-BOOMER AGE, I have a split list for what I'd still like to do in life. One is my list to do because I feel it is realistic, filled with things I can actually accomplish. The other list is more a pipe dream list; things I wish I could do but probably won't for sundry reasons.

My feelings about the latter list are probably not based so much on time constraints but on my "scaredy-cat" thinking. While I am impulsive to a degree, precautionary senses are always strong within me. Those senses are prevalent, as I like pain even less now than I ever have. Not *everything* I dream of would or could result in skinned knees, bruises, broken bones or bumpy falls, but I just don't do pain well.

What remains on my life's list to do are simple things, really. Traveling on a comfortable scale is my only requirement, although I wouldn't turn down grand-scale accommodations, should such be offered gratuitously. Comfort and enjoyment in everyday living, scaled to our simplistic requirements, are satisfactory and bring much happiness. My list of things to *really* try and do includes traveling and a number of pursuits that would bring me personal pleasure.

I want to see America. It would be nice to see other parts of the world, too. If only there were transatlantic roads bridging the continents, we could hook up our little travel trailer and tool over to tour Europe. What a blast! In the lower 48 states, I want to travel the state and county highways, tooling around the back roads. Mom-and-pop places, kitschy museums and well-known places are on my list. I want to ride the Oregon Trail, staying as true to the original one as the present route allows. Travel to visit family in New York is left to do. The lure of Broadway may prove too much, and I would disappear forever into those bright white lights. Vermont cousins would like for us to come there and live a whole year around.

(Husband says after the second 4-foot snow I would exit New England; however, I would love to experience the beauty of the area.) Husband is from the West Coast, and he left his heart there. We have family on the coast; mine are long-lost cousins whom I found on the Internet a few years ago. An extended trip to that area is a big dream for us.

The beauty and serenity of fly-fishing intrigues me, and I would love to learn. I think I could not pass up an opportunity to experience hang gliding or parasailing. Many years have passed since I have galloped across a green field on a horse. Just once again, I would love to ride like the wind.

Several years ago, Husband and I became "homesteaders." We moved into a rough one-room cabin in the foothills and are working toward improving what are now inconveniences of everyday living. A number of things are absolutely on my to do list: adding two rooms onto our cabin, developing a water system for our everyday use, enlarging our existing solar energy system, practicing permaculture, (planting within the environment as it is, not making a conventional garden), and creating an environmentally safe and pleasant home place.

Growing herbs, for food and medicinal purposes, has long been an interest and is now a passion of mine. I've only dabbled in this aspect of herb growing thus far, but I'm working toward larger-scale planting, growing and harvesting of herbs and spices. The sights, aromas and properties of tame and wild herbs and plants bring sensory satisfaction and delights into my jars and shelves. I am always learning and stand amazed at the properties contained in these wonderful plants.

My pipe dream list is a whole 'nother ball of wax.

The first thing that would help satisfy some of my other dreams is money. That's kind of crass, but it's necessary. I don't have any rich uncles left; actually I never had any of those anyway. Winning the lottery would be good although unlikely, since I only play it once every three months. I'm in the hole about $10, but one never knows.

Husband and I would buy a custom-built three-wheel cycle that would comfortably accommodate our aging, fluffy bodies. The design would include a compartment to hold our three four-legged children. Odd we would look but comfortable we would be on our road trips.

One of my dreams is to dress up in something long, flowing, purple and shiny to waltz with my husband — dressed in a tuxedo — across the floor of a beautiful ballroom. On the other end of that spectrum, we would gussy up in jeans and boots and tear up the dance floor of a Cajun zydeco club.

It makes me giddy to think about acting in a movie. I don't want to be the star ... well, I would if they asked me too, of course. My Southern accent can't be washed away with soap and water! My character would have to be Southern, for sure (with one of a number of regional accents I do). I would even settle for doing a voice-over; just put me in a movie!

The dream I feed on is being on a stage with a mic, entertaining and making an audience laugh. As much as I enjoy creating with the written word, my first love is verbal storytelling. While I have performed before small audiences, I still have to live through my 15 minutes of fame (hopefully more) before a much larger crowd.

In my youth, I had visions of living in a big house. As my age changed, interest and ideas of decorating styles and architecture of the house changed also. Eventually — and sensibly — I gave up on that. Even though I now live in a tiny cabin, I find my dream of living in a big house has not completely dissipated. This is evidenced in the "oohs and aahs" I utter when I see an impressive home that catches my eye. I would love to have all that room to ramble in, to use it to create different moods in which to write and just to be able to move about in all the spaciousness.

Some of my dreams, hopes, plans, wishes and schemes have fallen by the wayside, but I haven't forgotten them and would be ready and willing to forge ahead on a number of them if the opportunity presented itself.

In my dreams, I will bid adieu as I walk down a graceful winding staircase in my stilettos with a long dress floating out behind me and a beautifully beaded train following after me. With my hand on the baluster, I will slowly descend as I smile at the adoring crowd that eagerly awaits my repartee.

Always maintain a life's to do list. Never give up on your dreams, and hold your hopes high. I have. I do. I will.

By Derek Flynn

WHAT IS LEFT ON MY LIFE LIST TO DO? What do I still dream of? Going back to something that I touched on in the Spring essay about my 20-year-old self, I would ask: What if all the writing was never published and all the music never listened to? Would the creation of it have been a waste of time? This is what I like to call, "art for art's sake."

Traditionally, "art for art's sake" meant art that was created simply to be aesthetically pleasing but — supposedly — had no intrinsic worth beyond that. This was a 19th century notion at a time when art was seen as an agent for social change, when it was believed that art should be an educator and moral guide. The likes of Oscar Wilde rebelled against this and stated that art should be created simply "for art's sake" — for the simple act of creating.

So, my idea is a small twist on this. If I write for my whole life and the only place it ends up is the inside of my desk drawer, does that devalue the work as a piece of art? Similarly, if I create music all my life, but I'm the only one to hear it, does that devalue the work as a piece of music? Of course, these are extreme scenarios. The fact is, someone is going to see my writing and hear my music at some stage, but the question remains: Is the work any lesser because of it? And the answer? Of course not. We would do the work anyway, whether or not it was ever going to be seen.

Kafka went his whole life unpublished but for the odd short story. Now his books are regarded as masterpieces. Van Gogh sold one painting during his lifetime. Having said that, I've been writing music and prose for many years now; there have been times when they were heard and read by many people and times when they were heard and read by nobody. In the past six months, that's all changed. My music has been listened to and my writing read by more people than probably ever before. The reason? Very simple: the Internet and social media.

The democratization of the media by the Internet is nothing short of astonishing. Just take writing alone. These days, anyone can have a blog. Writing about politics is no longer the preserve of a small group of newspaper journalists; writing music or book reviews is no longer limited to the same few critics. This does bring up issues of quality control, of course, but the democratization of any media brings up those issues. That is the price we have to pay. At the end of the day, the opportunities afforded by such steps forward far outweigh any issues of quality control. After all, you can always change the channel.

Another example is filmmaking. There was a time when access to cameras and film editing equipment was impossible for the "ordinary" person. Now our phones capture high-definition video and our laptops can edit it to the level of a professional.

Starting a blog has opened up whole new avenues for me. Not only do I write, but I also post music on my blog. This means music that might have been sitting in a drawer can now be heard — and writing can be read. This is not to say that I don't still want that book publishing deal or record contract, it just means that it's not either/or anymore. It's not fame or obscurity. There's a new, exciting middle ground. The third option. The tools are all there.

So to answer the question of whether I have more life goals left to achieve: Of course. There are personal ones: to see new places, experience new things, laugh more and love more — all the things that any person wants. But there are creative ones, also: to make movies and books and music and send them out into the world. The tools are all there. All that's required is the imagination to create and the willingness to get up and do it, to not be afraid of failing or that someone won't like it. The world has changed and is changing; all that's required of us is the desire to create and the imagination to make it new.

By Jesse James Freeman

STARING INTO A BUCKET? I've done that lots of times, and although most of those times involved tequila, that's just not the kinda bucket I'm talking about this round. The bucket has become a metaphor for a keepsake container of all your hopes and dreams, bulleted and categorized so they can be checked off with a virtual highlighter wielded like a flaming angel's feather.

These are the things that I must accomplish before — well, you know — before I've run out of accomplishing stuff time. You ever tried to convince Lovely Rita from the little police golf cart to *not* give you a ticket? Arguing like you were that kid from the debate team you couldn't stand in high school while plugging quarters into that metal flashing totem on the sidewalk next to your car? Rita will shut you down. She will shake her head and silently judge you, and no matter if you're using your best lines or not, you will not woo her.

You can't win with her, because you're not supposed to. The universe is just not set up that way, and we're lucky that it's not. We're all on a schedule filled with day-to-day life events we have to accomplish to be an active and semirespectable member of society. There's no time to dream 24/7, otherwise, all we'd do is dream and our bucket would overflow quickly. Then all the really good stuff that we hold close that's really important for us to eventually accomplish would be suffocated by all the dumb stuff we toss into the bucket — just because.

I'm of the opinion that, over the years, the nature of what's prominent for us to accomplish changes, too. This is also a really good happenstance, because if the first stuff that I'd ever tossed in the bucket was all I had now, my life goals would be pretty shady and equally ridiculous.

For example: Own a fireworks hut, because then I'd have lots of fireworks and could blow stuff up whenever I want. Train to be a ninja, because then I'd have ninja powers and Kelly would notice me. Destroy Death Star, because then I'd have saved the galaxy and other-Kelly would be all into me. Learn to make my own bourbon in my bathtub while going to motorcycle repair school — but, secretly, kill vampires so other-other-Kelly would be really into me (yeah, there were three Kellys, and Kelly #3 was a real handful).

Point being, as we mature, the nature of our list must evolve. Otherwise, we become stuck on that boring road that Robert Frost got all bitchy about in that poem. I don't believe we can ever check everything off the list. Tragically, some people never check anything off their list. Some people never grow up, either (okay, maybe guilty), and their list remains polluted with dreams that aren't even their own.

Tons of people will tell you that their list has stuff on it like: live in a mansion and be rich and take supermodels out on yacht rides on some sea they've never heard of in some exotic locale they can't point to on a map, much less ever actually visit. I don't think those are their dreams. I think that is society telling you what to puke into your bucket.

I suppose I've simplified my dreams a lot since the days of wanting to be an astronaut/movie director in search of the elusive creature formed from the love union of the Loch Ness Monster and the wolf-man. I had to take a lot of that stuff off my list and re-evaluate.

I'd much rather enjoy quietly sitting on the shore of that far-away sea and watch that yacht with all the supermodels sail quietly by in the distance. I'd get a lot more thinking done that way, and I'd get to hear what the waves sound like and feel the sand between my toes. I can wait to shoot fireworks into the sky on July 4th and New Year's Eve, and the patterns of light against the dark will have much more meaning to me if I space it out a couple times a year like that. Both of the Death Stars got destroyed just fine a long time ago, and all three Kellys are in a galaxy far, far away. I tried my hand at being a ninja vampire killer, but I just couldn't breathe through that mask.

I've decided to leave the fancy stuff to characters I write about in books. I want to meet as many people as I can, and I want to be a good friend to them. I want to make them laugh — and I want them to make me laugh. I want to be true to myself and my family, and I

Autumn

want to spend the time that I have with them. I want to always keep learning and never stop being fascinated by new things. And anytime I stumble upon something cool and awe inspiring, I want to show the rest of the world — because I want them to feel that way, too.

That's pretty much all that's left in my bucket. It's harder than it sounds to scratch the rest of it off the list, but I'm working on it.

By Laura Kilmartin

EVERY YEAR, I TRAVEL with two of my best friends to the island of Nantucket for a long weekend of walking on the beach, biking through cranberry bogs and eating at restaurants that would make foodies from New York City and San Francisco weep with delight. To reach Nantucket, start at the port of Hyannis, Mass., wave to the Kennedy compound and hop on a ferry for a 30-mile, two-hour trip past the much larger and more populated Martha's Vineyard. When you disembark onto the rustic cobblestone street and find that bicycles outnumber cars, dogs outnumber people and scallop shells outnumber everything else, you know you have arrived.

My dream is to live on Nantucket someday.

While unremarkable to the untrained eye, Nantucket is as calm and relaxing an atmosphere as I've ever experienced. Physical changes manifest the moment I start breathing the Nantucket air. My blood pressure drops along with my heart rate and pulse. As someone who is a little tightly wound — and that's among the kinder phrases my friends have used — I spend my first days on the island feeling my shoulders relax from their normal tensed location of just under my ears into their more anatomically correct position. If I ever see my dream come true and move from annual visitor to resident, I might find myself relaxed right into a coma.

Since my first trip to Nantucket, it has been my goal to quit my job, move to the island and write. I can picture myself at my antique ship captain's desk, the sea breeze wafting through the facing window and a napping golden retriever curled at my feet. After writing a few pages of my upcoming novel — which is sure to be as critically acclaimed and financially successful as the last several written from this post — I'd hop on my Jessica Fletcher bike for a short break. Every day at the same time, I would dress in the island's accepted uniform of Nantucket red sweatshirt, khakis and deck shoes to cycle down the street, pick up my mail and a bouquet of wildflowers, and chat with the locals who have accepted me into their fold.

I even know the house I am going to buy when I move to the island. It is a stunning green Victorian dollhouse come to life, complete with a fully furnished front porch, gingerbread trim and the island's only gas streetlight standing sentinel outside as a beacon to guide me home. I've never been inside the house, but somehow I know it to be filled with upholstered window seats, built-in bookcases and Mr. Rochester sitting in the parlor with a decanter of brandy awaiting my arrival.

The house I dream of living in sits on one of the main streets of the lower village, up the road from the Brotherhood of Thieves pub and a stone's throw from my favorite bookstore. I've even seen wild bunnies frolic under the bushes on the front lawn. Walt Disney himself could not have created a more inviting setting.

I first laid eyes on my house during my maiden trip to Nantucket. I turned the corner from the rustic bed-and-breakfast where my friends and I were staying and found the house sitting there, just waiting for me. Admittedly, I don't know any details about my house. Who owns it? What is its history? I once briefly considered doing some research on the house but then worried that concrete proof of my house belonging to someone else who pays its taxes, cleans its gutters and calls the plumber when its toilet backs up would tarnish the magic.

I don't recall when the joke about this lovely residence being "My House" started among my girlfriends. It was probably that first day when I started snapping pictures of it, shocked that the exact house I'd sketched out with crayons as a little girl really existed outside a dream world. What's more, it existed on the magical island I had already grown to love.

For a time, we all just laughed at my one-sided love affair with this piece of real estate. But just as I'm not sure when the joking started, I don't remember exactly when it stopped and the belief became concrete that I had a real, organic connection to this house and its location. Make no mistake, but for the inconsequential matter of a deed with my name on it, I consider this property to be mine.

Absent any proof to the contrary, this behemoth of green and brown shingles can still belong to me. And it does. Every year I return to Nantucket and return to my house. I calculate how much taller the elm in the front yard has grown. I admire the new porch furniture with its brightly patterned cushions. And I dream. I dream of the novels I will write, the parties I will host and the way my ornaments will adorn the Christmas tree I plan to erect in the front window.

In those fleeting moments each year, my dream is a reality and my house on my calming island home truly belongs to me. And I belong to it.

By Marni Mann

THOUGH I HAVE ACCOMPLISHED so much professionally, there are still other areas that are important to me and so many personal goals I want to achieve. Writing has always been my passion, but to have my work published and read by a mainstream audience was simply a dream. I sampled many different genres before I realized my strength was dark, literary fiction, and I almost lost someone to addiction before I was inspired to write a novel-length piece. Three years ago, I wrote the first word of that book; last month it was published.

At this point in my life, my goal is to write two books a year. By the time I retire, I hope it takes a reader several minutes to scroll to the bottom of my Amazon page. It would be nice to have at least one of my novels opted for a movie and to see my characters given a face other than those I've created in my mind. One day, as I flip through the channels, I'd like to see the movie trailer of one of my titles playing on the TV, and I'd like to take my family to the premiere. It would be amazing if people listed Marni Mann as their favorite author, took the time to preorder my releases and kept a collection of my novels in their personal library.

I would like to study my craft more extensively under an author who has spent their career publishing novels. To learn what inspires them to write, where their stories come from, their process of completing a novel and their path to publication would make me a better writer. I want to remember their stories and teachings every time I sit down to write, and I want their words to influence the pieces I create, making me reach deeper to find that unique plot and character that's waiting to be born.

As I become more experienced and knowledgeable in writing, I would like to teach a course to undergraduates. My professors in college were experts at teaching the craft, not practicing its principles. If one of my professors had been a published fiction author, I believe

I would have graduated with a clear direction and an understanding of how to prepare myself for the publishing industry. After working with editors, collaborating with other writers and signing with a publisher, I have the insight to help students decide on a path and help them plan for a career in writing.

I've traveled throughout Europe, the Middle East, Canada, South America, Mexico and the Caribbean, but I would like to "see the world" — more of it. Traveling is a passion of mine. There's nothing like witnessing something so beautiful it takes your breath away: swimming in a body of water that's foreign to your skin, watching the sunset over eastern mountains, breathing in the different smells of ethnic cuisines. It's a full body experience that enlightens each of your senses, and it shows you there's beauty beyond words.

While spending time in Italy, I fell in love with the sexiness of Italians — their accent and the way they speak with their eyes when they talk to you. My dream is to become fluent in their language, which would require spending an extended period of time in Italy. I hope this comes true one day. I envision owning a villa in Tuscany and spending the summers there. I imagine sitting at a table overlooking the Mediterranean and sipping red wine while eating focaccia. That is my happy place. That is the inspiration an author needs to create their best work.

I have found great personal satisfaction in helping others, but with so many needs in our community, I would like to volunteer on a larger scale. By volunteering my time, I have witnessed the good that has come from my efforts. Whether it's working part time at the shelter, teaching children and adults how to read or mentoring prisoners, I want to give back to Sarasota, the city I call home. There are residents here who need guidance and a measure of hope. They need to believe there's more to life than their current situation. Addicts spend their days in a pitch-black existence, drained of their self-worth and believing that sobriety may be out of reach.

While I'm not an addict, I have witnessed the destructive nature of addiction — both physically and mentally — and I've studied the disease. I want to be a glimmer of hope to those who are fighting addiction. I want to help them search their desires, show them what they can accomplish once they reach sobriety and help them see that no one has to live in the dark.

I dream of becoming a mother. As I've gotten older, I've realized there's never a perfect time to have children. You can never fully prepare for the responsibilities of being a parent. You can never save enough money or be in the right career to allow a balance of equal time to your family and job. I've used my fair share of excuses: once we get back from this vacation; once the novel is written; once the sequel is complete; or after my birthday. I should put those excuses to rest. If I want to become a mother, there's only one way that's going to happen.

I dream of a day when addiction is a diagnosis, like cancer, and every addict has the opportunity to achieve sobriety. In that dream, appropriate medical treatments will be available to target the addict's tendencies, decision-making processes, urges and cravings. It will cure them of this disease. Rehab and counseling will be available nationwide, free of cost, and those who need help can receive it at any clinic or at specially designed hospitals that cater to addiction. I don't see an end to the war on drugs, but if we focus on addicts and addiction as much as dealers and distribution, there is a chance the demand for drugs won't be so high. And that would be a dream come true.

By Karla J. Nellenbach

WE ALL HAVE HOPES, DREAMS, goals, bucket lists. The things we want to say or do before we go down for the big dirt nap. Many are small, mostly attainable goals: find the love of your life, marry, have a family. Some are not so reachable: climb Mount Everest, wrangle unicorns, win the lottery. But still we hope that some (if not all) of these things will happen. Not only do we hope that we'll still be around to see them happen but that we'll be able to enjoy them as well.

I, like everyone else on this planet, have my own set of bucket list items — things I'd like to do, see, say or enjoy before the Reaper comes knocking on my door. Some of them are completely doable — small things that will make me smile. Others, admittedly, are not so easy, maybe even damn near impossible to complete. But I keep them on my list, just in case these lofty goals morph into reachable little gifts that are ripe for the taking.

So, lucky for all of you, fun friends, I'm going to share my list. Right here. Right now.

1. Visit the Emerald Isle. Every picture, postcard, documentary and movie I've ever seen that's been set in Ireland has been obscenely beautiful. I absolutely must see this mystical realm for myself. And who knows? I might even wrangle a unicorn while I'm there ... or, at the very least, catch a leprechaun and make him give up his lucky charms. Wink, wink.

2. Explore a shipwreck. Long before James Cameron made the *Titanic* cool, I was fascinated with documentaries about exploring the many famous shipwrecks in the world, the *Edmund Fitzgerald* being the most intriguing to me. To this day, I still want to see it.

3. Swim with dolphins. Pretty self-explanatory. And, really, I think everyone should do this at least once in their lifetime. Don't you?

4. Read seven books in seven days. I've actually already done this, but this should be a revolving bucket list item. Like, it should be done every few months or so.

5. Bicycle across an entire state. Granted, for me, this state might end up being Rhode Island, but how badass would it be to say that I rode a bicycle across an entire state? Exactly my point.

6. Survive the upcoming zombie apocalypse. Again, pretty self-explanatory. Because, really, don't we all want to do that?

7. Walk like an Egyptian. Yep, friends, I want to see the pyramids. Trek through the Valley of Kings where all the pharaohs from the New Kingdom are enshrined. Sail a boat along the Nile. See all there is to see of this part of the world. Note to self: BRING SUNBLOCK or else you will turn into a lobster within the first 10 minutes of your Egyptian tour. Skin cancer is so not on my bucket list.

8. Do something (big) for a complete stranger ... and not take credit for it. Because, hey, no one needs to know that, at heart, I'm just a big old marshmallow. I do have a reputation as a badass to uphold, after all.

9. Make enough money from my writing to support myself. I'm not talking pink Cadillacs, indoor swimming pools and a team of live-in nannies for my four-legged kids. Just enough to, you know, pay the bills and eat and stuff. That's the dream, right there. To eat.

10. Find buried treasure. This may walk hand in hand with number two on this list, but it needs to be added — just in case the shipwreck I explore has no hidden treasure trove of pirate booty. Knowing my luck, wherever I find this treasure, it will probably be cursed. I will scour the Earth searching for this bounty, and, when I find it, I shall battle against the hulking guardsmen who keep the treasure safe from looters like me. Then, I will emerge victorious, only to fall ill to some mysterious jungle fever — the unfortunate side effect of cursed objects everywhere. Which is probably why this list stops at number 10. Hello? If I do end up with a cursed object on my hands, I won't be around much longer to complete any more of the list. Am I right, or am I right?

As far as life and bucket lists go, yours is only as good, as entertaining or as enjoyable as you want it to be. Aiming for infinity (and beyond) doesn't necessarily mean that you'll fail. It just ensures that you will always be striving for more. And isn't that what our time here is for?

I think Kurt Vonnegut said it best with: *Of all the words of mice and men, the saddest are, "It might have been."*

For me, I want to be able to look back on my life and not only be proud of the many things I've done but also of the things that I tried, whether I accomplished them or not.

Autumn

By Terry Persun

I REMEMBER STANDING IN MY FLANNEL SHIRT with my hip cocked and my arms hanging loosely at my sides. In my best cowboy drawl, I said, "Git on yer horse and head outta town before sundown." I kept my eye on my brother's right hand. If he made a play for his gun, I was ready. I knew I could draw faster than he could, but only if I saw it coming. I wasn't going to let him win this time.

"I'm not leavin'," he said. And at that moment, he blinked, shifted his weight and went for it.

I drew my pistol and snapped off several caps.

That was only the beginning of the roles that I would play. There were also captains in the army, crazy scientists, disgruntled family members, shopkeepers and teachers. I have always enjoyed taking on other roles.

Even now, I can quickly shift into the mannerisms of a ship's captain or a lawyer, a hick from the country or a top executive from a big corporation. Embodying the physical movements of a person from my imagination and taking on their attitudes, grammar and syntax, is something that comes easily to me. Acting like someone else — male, female or alien — is why I turned to writing in the first place. I can shift from personality to personality, from page to page. I can give inanimate objects feelings and make people cold and calculating.

Writing allows me to explore my personal beliefs, moral boundaries and attitudes about anything and everything. Since I've always been interested in many subjects, I find that writing provides me with the license to research whatever I want — no excuses or reasons necessary. And I get to explore how others might think and feel and act under dire circumstances, even if it's not how I might act.

While writing a historical novel about a mulatto passing as white, I researched a time period outside my own. I got to explore the attitudes of race from multiple points of view. In researching the area of the country where I grew up, I was able to relive moments of my childhood, like playing in the woods along the West Branch of the Susquehanna River. I also learned what life was like in a logging town, which is where my grandfather had grown up. I had heard stories, but my research brought things into perspective.

Through my writing, I've taken on the persona of a man dying of cancer. And rather than focus on the horrible parts of the disease, the hospital visits and medications, I stepped into how the man chose to change his relationships with his family members before he died. Within the pages of my books, I've had the opportunity to explore the link between creativity and madness and to embody an advertising executive who goes on a Native American vision quest. I've gone through a devastating divorce in one and lived through a woman who gave up her children in another. I've designed a dystopian/utopian world, built a time machine and explored another planet with intelligent life.

I can — and do — explore whatever interests me. As my mom always used to say about me, I'm always running amuck — either physically or mentally.

I have a fairly full life, but that doesn't mean there aren't more things I'd like to explore — outside of my writing. Although I've traveled to other planets in my stories, I'd like to travel to more countries on this planet. I have taken flying lessons, so that I know how it feels to take off and land a plane, but it might be nice to actually get my pilot's license. I'd love to have the time to take more college courses, perhaps in archeology and marine biology or physics and philosophy. It would be great to spend several summer months on an island exploring the indigenous plants and animals — and writing every day. I enjoy time alone and time spent creating, so I can imagine spending more time sculpting, painting or playing an instrument.

And let's not forget my family. I love to explore new cities with my wife, museums with my daughter and hiking trails with friends. As much as there are things I'd like to do before I die, I think spending time with people I enjoy is probably at the top of the list.

Autumn

Regardless of how long my list might be or how much running amuck I might wish to do, I must admit that I enjoy what I do now — and would simply like to do more of it. So, when I think of what is left to do in life before I die, the list could go on forever, but it could just as easily stop right here, right now, at this very moment.

By Laura Tiberio

WHAT HAPPENS TO A DREAM DEFERRED? Well, I can think of at least three possibilities.

Option one: It winds up shoved in the back corner of my mind, sleeping among dust bunnies and that hideous blue eye shadow I used to wear in seventh grade. And just like that makeup, I remember the dream fondly now and again — but it never sees the light of day.

Option two: It plants itself deep in the fertile plans of my imagination. Over time, it grows strong and leafy on all of the would-ofs, could-ofs and should-ofs. Its fronds begin tickling at my conscious mind until I am finally forced to see the dream in all its blooming glory. Then, of course, I am faced with the task of deciding between prized flower (to be cherished and nurtured) or invasive weed (to be rooted out and stamped into a slimy green paste beneath my heel).

Option three: It winds up on a list.

I don't know about you, but I make lists. Some of my lists are quick and dirty, penned on the back of an envelope with a broken crayon sort of thing. These are meant only for short-term keeping; they include errands, things to buy at the grocery, the number of times my mother has called. Other lists are for use and reuse. These might be laminated cardstock charts (did I mention I love clip art?) or spreadsheets on the computer. (If you find this latter idea compelling and wish more information on how to make your very own, I will put you in contact with my husband or various members of his family. They, being of the engineering persuasion, have an entirely different level of commitment to lists.) These short-term lists are for keeping my household running. Who feeds the cat? What time is the doctor appointment? When did I last bathe? (This question is on a list generally reserved for my children. We have a saying in my family: If you can't remember when you took your *last* shower, it's probably time to take your *next* one.) But I digress, as I do quite often, actually — which is why I have so many lists. I do what I can to help my Swiss-cheese brain.

But some lists are for keeps. And these are the kind I like to write on fancy paper with a nice pen and keep in a special place. These lists include the hilarious things that 3-year-olds say, that amazing wine we drank on our fifth anniversary, the names of authors whose books have touched my heart, names of friends I haven't seen in so long and want to see again, and what my children wore on their first days of kindergarten. Memories. Hopes. Passions. Dreams.

I also have a list of things I want to do before I die. This list cannot be found with a computer mouse or sandwiched between the pages of a baby book. Sure, hints and fragments of this list are found scattered about the house, in the backseat of the car or tucked under the bed. But to see this list in its entirety, you have to look inside my head.

What is on this list? Hard to say. It changes daily — sometimes even twice before breakfast. Sometimes things I thought had long been tossed will show up again and take what they see as their rightful place at the head of the line. Occasionally, I will have one of those gray, bleary days where nothing on the list seems remotely possible. Then the sun comes out, and I see my list through rose-colored rays — and everything is back on the menu.

So, what *kinds* of things are on the list? Oh, the usual stuff, to be sure. Things like: write a witty Christmas letter where everyone in my family has either gone to Harvard, been awarded a Nobel Prize or cured some horrific disease. Or sail around the world in a wooden sailboat built by my husband in his fabulously outfitted shop. (Wait, how did that get on *my* list?). Then there are things like: win the lottery, travel the world and donate to charity.

OK, maybe the list includes some more *realistic* usual stuff. Go some place tropical and bring my kids so they can swim in a *warm* ocean. Drink a really nice bottle of wine. Complete a triathlon (it could be a short one.) Spend a weekend in Paris. Learn to dance the tango — really well. Actually print out the good digital pictures (and delete the bad ones.) Have hair like Rita Hayworth (at least for a day.) Watch all the *Star Wars* movies with my son. Climb a mountain with my daughters.

This list also includes some not-so-usual stuff. Like figure out how to download music onto my daughter's iPod before she can do it herself. Clean out my mother's shed and keep her from filling it up again. Convince my husband that just because he "could build that" doesn't mean he should.

And then there's the heavy stuff. I dream of forming good relationships with my children that will survive their transformation into adults. I want to live so long that I might see my children grow up, reach their own goals and dreams, and have children of their own — but not so long that I outlive them. I want to make a final, lasting peace with so many of the decisions I have made, especially the ones that seem to bubble up at the most inconvenient times and insist on yet another round in the ring so they can work me over, cause more self-doubt and tear open old wounds. To perfect the art of being in the moment and not allow the ghosts of the past or the terrors of the future to detract from the magic of now, so that time can feel savored and not spent. To see the beauty in all things, and to do so clearly and with such sharp focus on the beauty that any flaws become character to my eyes.

And at the very end of my days, I hope for clarity of mind, calmness of soul and lightness of spirit — and a really nice pen to check it all off my list.

By Laura Zera

ON A GOOD DAY, I feel like I have limitless time to do all the things I want to do in my life. Other days, I am overwhelmed by low-grade panic and think, "My list is too long! I'll never get it all done." Then I wonder if that intermittent pain behind my left ear is a brain tumor or if the guardian angel who protects me on my travels has taken a vacation of his own. My morbid preoccupation with plane crashes doesn't help. And what if that palm reader at the fair was myopic and the long lifeline she saw was really just dirt?

I'm 43. That's about halfway through, I figure — as long as I keep taking my fish oil supplements and look both ways before entering an intersection. There are no guarantees, though. Somebody might decide that my number is up long before I do. (In addition to a life list, I'm also working on an exit strategy). So what to do, what to do? Well, the plan is to cover all the things on my list and enjoy the journey, however long it may last. I'll continue to save money for retirement but spend some of it now on tickets (plane/concert/speeding), classes, pets and people. The bottom line is to have a complete and utterly good time (minus the commemorative tattoo — I'm a baby when it comes to needles). Now for a few items that are on the list...

Wandering the globe is like the blood in my veins: vital. Antarctica is my last unvisited continent; it's on my list partly because I'm fascinated that such a place can even exist. There are deterrents to getting there, though: the steep cost and equally steep per-person vomit ratio whilst traversing the Drake Passage. But those factors are far outweighed by the unparalleled opportunity to spend days with a dedicated naturalist while learning about wildlife, geology, oceanography and glaciology — and then to see these amazing things firsthand. Plus, I have a major thing for penguins.

I also want to go on a big adventure with my big sister: cooking school in Italy or a safari in Africa. We've never gone anywhere together — not even to Disneyland or for a weekend in Las Vegas.

My sister and I need to get pooped on by pigeons in Piazza San Marco (it's very stylish Italian poop) or have our campground raided by baboons in Botswana.

Even though I can practically feel my cerebral mass shrinking with each year that passes — it even squeaks when I think too hard — I still have a great desire for further formal education. When I was working with a career coach a handful of years ago, she asked why I wanted a graduate degree. "All the cool kids are doing it," I said. The driving force then was that I felt I needed it to stack up to the competition. Admittedly, I still bump up against the icky feeling that I have something to prove; however, the driving force now is that I really want to learn — to dive deeply into an area of study and see how my experienced, adult brain and soul would work its way through new and challenging material.

Mastering a second language is forever on my list. I started with Ukrainian at the age of 8 after discovering a book in my mother's den; the Cyrillic alphabet really threw me for a loop, and I quickly gave up. After a stint on an Israeli kibbutz in 1987, I took lessons in Hebrew. Although "give me a kiss" and "I'm hungry" were about as far as I got, for some strange reason I still sometimes count in Hebrew in my head. Started Spanish. Stopped Spanish. And, despite four years of high school French and two extended stints in Francophone countries, I haven't bagged that one, either. I refuse to point to Pig Latin and call it good. There has to be a way.

There are lots of other fun and crazy things on the list, too. Some are more audacious than others. I'd like to have a third go at working in international development for a nonprofit organization. (There's absolutely nothing to rival a business meeting that takes place while you're barefoot and cross-legged on the floor of a village chief's hut.) I want to be the news, traffic and weather girl who chit chats between songs with the morning-show DJ on a rock-n-roll radio station. My friend Darlene and I envision opening a no-kill animal shelter (although she doesn't realize that she'd get stuck doing all the work while I played with the animals). I hope to establish residency with my husband in a warm locale in the southern hemisphere and drop off the big-city grid for part or all of the year. And, of course, I want to keep writing. Yes, I do fantasize about having a best seller one day. I know it won't make me a better person, but I want it anyway.

There's something else, too. It's probably the most significant thing on my list.

I long to wake up each morning and feel like I am exactly where I am meant to be, doing exactly what I need to be doing. It's true that setting goals and having a life list are sure-fire ways to boost one's chances of actually doing some of those things — in fact, we sell ourselves short if we don't. While it never hurts to create a vision and think big in terms of what we want in our lives, what I truly seek is the inner peace that comes from being happy right where I am, even on the days when my biggest accomplishment is getting all the wax out of my dog's ears. (She has the deepest, narrowest ear canals ever). Even if I never do a single thing that is spelled out on my life list, I want to be okay with that.

For me, getting to that place is a tougher road to travel than finishing a graduate degree or making the trip to Antarctica a reality. It doesn't take the regular dollop of brains, money and ingenuity; it takes the transformational step of learning to be best friends with my soul. To fully accept and love myself, even on my most rotten, stupid, ugly days. To be able to take those rotten, stupid, ugly days and deftly turn them into entirely pleasant days. To feel that things are perfect, exactly as they are.

Sometimes I think this could all take a while. And sometimes the inner voice kicks in and snipes: "You're 43. How could you not have this figured out, you dolt?" That's okay, though. Antoni Gaudi's Sagrada Familia has been under construction in Barcelona for 130 years, but that doesn't make it any less valuable. Truly, my life is like a manuscript: the first draft was pretty crappy, but the revisions keep getting better, and my life list helps to develop an exciting plot.

I'm 43. I'm only halfway through.

By Tracey M. Hansen, Co-Author

I'VE TALKED ABOUT THIS BEFORE, but my "life list" is ever changing. Everyone has a bucket list. Whether it's kept in your head or scribbled on a napkin in your nightstand drawer, that list is a constant force that drives most of us. So, what's on my bucket list? Oh, you know...

I'd like to have a baby. At every visit, my gyno asks me if I'm planning to have children. I smile and say, "Yes, but not yet." She then raises an eyebrow and proceeds to lecture me on the passage of time and my body's abilities. Then she likes to throw these words at my head: advanced maternal age. She makes me feel like the British woman on the Discovery Channel who got IVF at 63. I'm 30! And in this bitch's eyes, I may as well be 130. Basically, what she's telling me is that every passing month I'm that much closer to being shriveled up inside. Every moment that goes by will make me more likely to be at my child's first play in an auditorium filled with parents straight from the set of *Teen Mom*. So, to me, having a baby is a goal; to my gyno, it's a fucking deadline. I swear she is two appointments away from telling me to use it or lose it.

Get married. To me this is both a goal and a deadline. I want to get married to ManPal sooner rather than later, because I don't want to be an old bride. I think he's finally starting to listen to the subliminal messages I whisper to him at night, because the other night he whispered back, "Go to sleep." Baby steps people. I don't want to wait until I'm much older, because nothing goes together worse than a sparkly strapless princess ball gown ... and crow's feet.

Sing solo karaoke. I cannot carry a tune in a bucket and will never be on the *American Idol* stage (without security being called to remove me), so I figure this is the next best thing. I did sing a solo once in a play at the Jewish summer camp where mom signed up me and my sister. We were raised Catholic, but the temple was closer to the house than the church. I was awesome — I think.

Autumn

Run the New York City Marathon. Thanks to the video my sister made of my triumphant cross at the finish line, my attempt at a half marathon can be seen over and over again. I am still trying to edit out the little boy's voice so that you don't hear him shout, "Look, Mommy. She's dead last!" And if Al Roker can run the marathon in eight hours, just call me Hussein Bolt, because I think I can do it in, like, seven hours and 45 minutes — give or take an hour or two.

I want to be on the *Today* show — without them having to interview me from inside my prison cell. I'm thinking more along the lines of when they turn my book (you know, the one that's going to be a number one *New York Times* best seller?) into a movie. Matt Lauer will interview me, telling me I have pretty eyes and complimenting my outfit, and we will live happily ... what was I saying?

I want to teach. Maybe for a day, maybe for a year — however long it would take them to realize I shouldn't be within 500 feet of a school. Sometime in my life, I would like to teach creative writing ... or maybe wood shop. I can make a badass name keychain like nobody's business. Also, I saw an alarming post recently on the wall of one of my Facebook friends. After teaching his first day of ninth grade English, he posted this: "Made it threw my first day." If anything, I think I can improve our educational system, because I certainly don't think I can make it any worse. P.S. — My kids are going to private school, because if this guy is still teaching, my kids won't even be able to identify the letters in their alphabet soup.

I want to be involved with a restaurant. I am fascinated by how they work and run. Granted, I have never done anything at a restaurant besides shovel food in my face and indulge in too many vodka-vodka's. I have never been a waitress or hostess, never bused a table and never made dinner for more than six people, but I feel fairly confident in my abilities to do all of it. I'm sure it would be a phase that I would get over pretty quickly — after seeing exactly how the food is made, enduring an angry guest yelling at me and having to clean unidentifiable glop off of the floor. Never mind. I just talked myself out of it.

I want to learn to speak French. As a woman of the world, I will need to know how to tell people off in multiple languages. I live in Florida, so Spanish makes way more sense. But French sounds sexy — and I've never been one for practicality. Besides, when I go to Canada to visit my relatives, I can practice my knowledge of French by reading the words on the container of milk-in-a-bag.

Oh, and I want to learn the piano so I can play the "tiger" song from *The Hangover*. Doesn't everyone?

—WTYM

Winter

*What would you want said
about you on your 80th birthday?*

By Tess Hardwick, Co-Author

THE WOODS ARE HUSHED HERE along the creek. It is mid-winter now, and the trees and mountains above are white against an unadorned blue sky on this morning of my 80th birthday. The sun glints on the water as I shuffle along, and I pause for a moment to listen to the gurgle of water between stones. I walk every day — sometimes on foot, other times on snowshoes — still seeking clarity. And now, after a lifetime of practice, the *source* is evident: God always meets me here in the stillness.

The snow is fresh today, light and dry. It's the kind my daughters would have loved to hold in their hands and sculpt. But their creations would not have lasted, as nothing does in this life. What we are left with in the end is simply the joy we found in the doing.

My hands and body are not as agile as they once were, having given in to the inevitable unfolding. But my mind is clearer, and there is still work to be done. The brisk air has cleared my mind, leaving it as a fresh piece of canvas, and my desk waits. I thought I would be quiet now, less driven, with a peace about me that might allow a day to go by without work. Yet I find there is still more to say. As the years turn one after the other, there is always something new I've learned, some angle of repose unseen the year before. All of my experiences have merged into this collective wisdom. Each pain and sorrow and triumph, every observation and remembrance, is focused by time and reflection.

This afternoon, there will be a party in my honor. At each birthday, my husband and I look at one another and wonder if this will be the last one together. We make jokes about it, always laughing but knowing the end is near. He's an old man now, and I'm an old woman; we're a matched set this way. I'm shorter (which I didn't think was possible), and he's stooped slightly at the shoulders (perhaps from the burdens he carried during the early years of our family). We're gentle with one another now, in our last years. The adjustment of young love and the stress of middle-aged striving are long since gone; we are left with just the gentle presence of a known love.

My daughters will come, thriving and beautiful in their middle age. And my breath will catch at the sight of them. The privilege of being their mother is the deepest joy of my life. I will think of their childhood faces, able to recall them in an instant. My own mother said she could still see the child I once was, even as I said goodbye to her in the late autumn of my own life. I think of her, on this day of my birth, missing her. Even though I'm an old lady, the pain of her loss is still fresh to me, for when I think of her, I am a child — safe and loved — touching her warm skin near the river.

Now, I bring my weathered hand to my heart as my eyes search the peaks of the mountains for her presence. I feel her there. I feel my father, too, and all the loved ones already departed. I know they all hover just beyond my sight and wait for my arrival from this world to the one God prepares for me.

But this afternoon, my daughters will bring new life: my grandchildren, still in the flushed dewiness of spring. They ease the pain of losing those who've gone before and the disappearing years of my own life, for this is the cycle, the circle.

There are a few of us still here from the old days. "A few old birds," I tell them, when we laugh together over the phone. And the birds will come, some hobbling up the steps but still able to pour a glass of rich red wine and toast the years God's given us on this earth.

In the early afternoon, car after car arrives in our long curving driveway. "The inn is full," Emerson tells me. "Every room taken." There are writers, artists and musicians of every age that I've welcomed into my heart and life over the years. And book people — everywhere. They've all come to raise a glass. Those who remain are still louder than we should be for people our age, and the party grows lively. My daughters have thought of everything. Twinkling lights are strewn in the trees around the patio, and the sounds of music and clinking glasses fill the room. Dave has prepared slow-cooked pork on his barbeque, claiming: "It hasn't killed us yet, so how about one more time, for old time's sake?"

At some point, Ella makes a clinking sound on her glass, and everyone gathers around to give a toast. (This will feel embarrassing and wonderful all at once.)

Ella begins with the story of my first novel and the initial rejections, of the time I cried on the bathroom floor. And then, how I scrambled up from the floor and went back to work. She tells of seeing me in the early mornings at my desk, pounding away at the keyboard, doing something I loved. "She taught us that," she says. Then, she recalls me quoting my grandfather, who lived to be 87: "You must always do something, it doesn't matter what it is." She tells the crowd of my closeness to God, of my daily prayers and my vigilant daily meditation. And I whisper, under my breath, so that only she can hear: "You gave me that."

"My grandfather, we called him Papa, used to say my mother could light up a room," Emerson says. I think of my father's own smile, and then of Emerson, smiling at 5 weeks old. "I was merely reflecting what I saw in his face and yours," I will tell her later. Next, Emerson shares my secret longing: "She always wanted to be a source of light and hope to everyone around her. And she has done that."

I weep, knowing all the times I failed and thinking of moments of despair and anger and doubt. Yet this, this declaration from my daughter, is *something*. It's an indication, perhaps, that I was closer than I thought.

"She's provided an adventure," Dave says, with red-rimmed eyes. He doesn't finish, embarrassed to say what he means, what is deep inside from a lifetime of loving the same woman. But I know. I have always known.

One after another the guests share stories. They use words like inspired, defended and encouraged — all of which are probably only half-truths — to describe my kindness and generosity. I soak it in, grateful they think I've mattered. Some of the old birds tell of how hard we've laughed together while others speak of my devotion during both good times and bad.

I look around the room at those who remain and then out to the mountain once again to those already gone. I fill with love until I think I might burst, knowing these relationships have meant the most to me — far more than all my yearnings and ambitions.

After everyone leaves and Dave goes to bed, I pad down the hall to my office, walking slowly now and being careful not to slip. I sit at my desk, reflecting on this moment in time and of what I know could be the last birthday celebration of my life. The walls of my office are covered with my life: family and friends in photos, remembrances of my travels, book covers and writing awards. Still, I know it is not the past that matters but the present. There is still work to do. But it will wait until tomorrow.

Then, as I'm leaving the room, I notice a wrapped gift from Emerson on my reading chair in the corner. It is her work, a painting of my favorite stretch of beach on the Oregon coast. Below the image, carved into the wooden frame, is my mantra, the words I've tried to live by: "Begin with gratitude. Dream big. Take risks. Work hard. Don't give up. Pay it forward. End with gratitude."

Reminded, I fall upon my knees. "Thank you," I say.

In our bedroom, Dave is asleep, snoring softly. I pull the covers up to my chin and reach for his warmth with my foot. He shifts slightly and comes closer. "Did you leave the window open?" he asks.

"Yes," I say.

Dave claims we've lived so long and well because we sleep with the window slightly open, even on the coldest nights. Wide-awake, I stare out the open window. It begins to snow, and the light from the patio illuminates each individual flake. I think of my father. I remember the night so long ago, my little girl hand in his.

No one flake is the same; each is perfect in its uniqueness. For that I am grateful.

WRITE FOR THE FIGHT

By Gordon Bonnet

WHAT WOULD I LIKE PEOPLE TO SAY about me on my 80th birthday? Well, the first thing that comes to mind is, "Wow, he looks damn sexy in those swim trunks ... he can't be a day over 30, can he?" But I guess that given the number of laugh lines and white hairs I have at 51, that may be a little unrealistic.

So staying in the realm of the marginally likely, let's start with, "Happy birthday! You're still alive and in good health! How fortunate that you still have your vision, hearing and as much in the way of mental faculties as you ever had!"

But what will I be thinking on that day, 29 years from now?

Mostly that no one makes it that far in isolation or accomplishes what they do without a far-reaching network of support. The myth of the self-made man is just that: a story, a fiction. I would not have been the teacher I was without the mentorship of my colleagues, guidance from thoughtful administrators, and the patience and humor of thousands of students who were willing to sit still and listen to what I had to say for an hour a day for 180 days.

I would not have been the musician I was without the encouragement of people like Kathy, who, when I told her that I was honored by the invitation to join her band but didn't think that I was good enough, said to me: "Perhaps you've misunderstood. The correct answer was, 'Yes, that'd be *lovely*. I'm thrilled to join your band.'"

I wouldn't have become the writer I was without the support of people like Alex, who told me in complete seriousness one day, "I'm looking forward to being able to tell people, 'I used to have dinner with Gordon once a week and discuss writing. And that was *before* he got famous.'"

I can't imagine having made it at all without the steadfast friendship of people like my cousin, Carla, who dealt with my periodic descents into the Slough of Despond with a gentle suggestion that I better get myself together and stop feeling sorry for myself or she'd fly up to New York to personally kick my ass. Her messages always left me laughing and able to say with honesty that she could cancel her plane reservations, that I already felt better.

It's the connections that matter — much more than any presumption of my being able to look back from the lofty edifice of octogenarianism and celebrate fame and fortune won from my music or my writing. If, at my 80th birthday party, I'm simply surrounded by the people who've been part of my life for eight decades — my fellow musicians and writers, friends, family members and other loved ones — that will be plenty.

Still, I can imagine a few heartfelt messages from the nearest and dearest. I've never been much of a prognosticator, but I can give it a shot. So raise a glass of your favorite libation with the three people who've meant the most to me:

From my older son: "Here's a toast to the birthday boy. You always kind of wondered if I'd make it, didn't you? Back when I was younger, you didn't think my fire and idealism could last. And now I'm an environmental lobbyist — so it all kind of worked out, didn't it? I'm happy and settled, and we still have lunch together every weekend and discuss philosophy. It's all good. Love you, dad ... you've always been there for me, even when I was a pain-in-the-ass teenager. I want you to know how much that means to me. Oh, yeah — and see me after the party. I've got some more music suggestions for you."

From my younger son: "Yo, Papa. Who'd a thought? You're 80. Dear God, that's old. But then, I'm 50 ... I can't believe that, either. Hey, you remember how I always used to leave my stuff all over your classroom? I now have art students who do the same thing in my studio. I guess it's only fair, right? And were you telling the truth when you said you still have every piece of artwork I ever gave you? Even the goofy-looking little clay totem I made when I was in second grade? Hard to believe. Anyway, happy birthday. I made you a great big ceramic coffee mug for your birthday; clearly the one you have is too small."

From my wife: "Wow, honey. Eighty years old! And we've been together for, what is it, 38 years now? Amazing. It's only gotten better, our time together — hasn't it? Traveling, music, art, laughter and love. Always lots of love — even during the hard times and the dry spaces when everything seemed like it was a struggle. When work was a drag, when time together was a few minutes here and there, grabbed when we could. But now ... both retired and time to play. Pretty cool, isn't it? And I hope you've been taking your vitamins, because tomorrow we leave for a month to go on a trip, poling a raft up the Yangtze River. So, a toast: Here's to another 38 years of adventures."

By Galit Breen

I STAND BY MY HUSBAND'S SIDE and lace my fingers with his.
My hands are weathered from travel and teaching and motherhood. He doesn't mind.
Twinkle lights and candlelight color this room of celebration, from plush carpet to open windows.
It's the night of my 80th birthday.
My children are tall and grown and woven into their own lives, but we are still tethered as five and tightly bound by our shared stories.
They each speak, their cheeks raised and eyes lit, as their adult voices lilt words that I penned so many years before, when they were so very young.
"She was a friend," the reading begins with Kayli, her cocoa eyes serious, focused.

Our Keds rest neatly on the seats in front of us, a row of white canvas toes lined up in indisputable youth. We pull our pegged-jean knees to our chests and wrap our arms around them.

Our hair falls loosely onto our shoulders. We whisper urgently, laugh freely.

My tweed seat leans farther back than I expect, and, just as the lights dim, I start. This breathes new life to our giggles.

Blushing, our teachers walk around the circular auditorium shushing, hovering, reminding.

Faint Pink Floyd notes surround and then finally silence us all.
The lights twinkle.
The music envelops.
My friends make this moment sweeter.

I was 15 years old and had never taken in the night sky, inside or out. My parents and I took many walks, visited numerous gardens and traveled a staggering amount.

But the sky remained an unexplored mystery to me. A gift that I had no idea needed opening.

"She was a wife," Chloe's familiar voice continues, sweeping a caramel lock behind one ear.

Many moons later, Jason and I stumble out of bed in the middle of the night. I have just finished pulling my hair into a messy ponytail as he laces his fingers with mine. "Come on, we need to get going." He pulls me along, rushing me out the bathroom door.

Less than a year together, and I was struck by how anxious he was to be on time, to not miss out. This imaginary Post-It note has been endlessly helpful throughout our life together.

We wrap ourselves in thick, gray sweatshirts and GAP jeans. We fill our Starbucks mugs with rich hot chocolate the color of fresh spring soil warmly muted by skim milk and whipped cream.

We drive through the night feeling a kismet connection with the few others on the road. Are they looking for an open space, too? Is the meteor shower calling their name, as well?

Finally parked, we gracelessly climb atop our leased Jetta. We sit with a ridiculously thick quilt resting on our knees, hot chocolate warming our hands. My head leans on his shoulder, and we breathe in this magic.

Still air.

Bright twinkles.

Hope and shine and pure and clean and untouched and never-knew-it-could-bes.

"She was a mother," Brody says as he steps forward, shoulders back and chin tilted, a mirror image of his father.

Tonight we are hurried. Jason and I, along with our three children, arrive home after an evening of eating too much and staying out too late.

We feel the bedtime push and are dangerously close to meltdowns and tears, yells and frustrations.

But when Brody pads onto the driveway and asks, "Where's the moon?" from behind his pacifier, we pause.

We take in his almost-a-boy stance. His words that ring just right, too big. His titch-too-long bright blond hair falling into his eyes. Neither one of us says no.

And, yes, we are the type of parents who too often fall into the traps of "not tonight," "maybe later" or "this too can wait." But we understand the draw of a night sky and moments that fleet.

So, we trudge through itchy grass into our backyard and step into the sweet spot between the tall trees of the woods and the warm light of our home.

We place Kayli between us. Her head rests against my shoulder. Jason and I each hold another child up high, as high as we can reach. And as a family, we look up at the stars, the moon, the magic.

We breathe in this moment, this gift. It is opened.

"She was a writer," Jason says in closing, his hand still wrapped in mine.

I hold their words at the edge of my heart.

They are versions of my own that I've shared with them throughout our years together.

These are their stories to tell now, gifts to be opened another day.

Because now, it is time for chocolate cake and sparkly champagne — the way all big moments are meant to be celebrated.

By F. Jo Bruce

WHAT DO I WANT TO HEAR on my 80th birthday?

"What? She's 80? My gosh, she doesn't look a day over 60."

My husband saying, "You still make me hot, baby," and knowing that he means it.

"Her memory is still clear as a bell on a cold winter's night."

"Ma'am, your eye test was good, your coordination is sharp and you are an excellent driver. Your new license is good for 10 years. Have a nice day."

"So, I hear you and your hubby are entering the dance marathon again this year. Might as well take the trophy home for the fifth year in a row."

"I'm so glad I took your aerobics class. You are a wonderful instructor."

From my hairdresser: "Your hair is so thick, I'm not sure I can style it exactly like this picture."

"Not everyone can wear this particular style, but it looks fabulous on you."

"Oh, my goodness, you did a beautiful job on this quilt, stitches so tiny and even. You're starting another one?"

"You don't have a single hair on your chinny-chin-chin."

"Can you believe that little old lady just knocked the crap out of a dude for saying, 'Outta my way, grandma, I'm in a hurry.'"

"When she says she's so happy she could turn a cartwheel, she ain't joking, is she?"

"You cooked all of this? By yourself? Wow!"

"I love your high heels. They make your legs look great."

"I'm sorry, ma'am, you have to be 65 in order to receive the senior discount."

"You are the best grandmother ever."

"You are going to be as spectacular a great-great-grandmother as you were a granny and a mom."

"You have always wanted to slide down that banister, haven't you? You can take that off your bucket list now."

"So round, so firm, so fully packed, and, baby, you are still so stacked!"

"Oh, my gosh, I can't stop laughing. That lady told that man to 'jump up a wild man's ass' when he bumped her car."

"Mom, your sewing was so beautiful. People thought our clothes were ready-made."

"Granny, my friend said you were the cutest granny he had ever seen."

"When I get old, I want to be just like you."

"When you are sweet, you are really sweet, but when you are mad, you are a bitch!"

A former schoolmate saying, "I would have recognized you anywhere by your eyes and smile."

Mom/Granny/Sis/Lady, remember when…

"…you took all the grandkids, to Disney World — by yourself!"

"…you made up a routine to strip music and performed it for us — but with your clothes on, thank goodness."

"…you made dozens of chocolate chip cookies for our bake sale and forgot to put in the chocolate chips?"

"…you stayed up four days straight when we all came down with the flu at the same time?"

"…you performed a C section on that pregnant stray cat we brought home?"

"…those kids across town whose mama died and you made dresses for the little girls and shirts for the boys? Then you cooked Thanksgiving dinner for them with *our* turkey and we had to eat fried chicken."

"…Daddy dug a hole in the backyard and later you let us put water on the dirt and have a mud fight? We thought you were the coolest mom in town."

"…the night Mrs. V came to the house drunk and wanted you to pray for her, and you said, 'Lord, please make this sot drunk disappear from this house before I kill her. Amen.'"

"...the little lessons you always taught us, like 'pretty is as pretty does; do unto others; always return a favor with a kindness; and if you get in trouble at school, you will get into worse trouble at home.'"

At my grand party on my 80th birthday, family and friends would say they loved me and desired to be with me — until I was raising hell about something and then they'd want to give me a wide berth.

Of course, I would love praise and flattery, but, in all honesty, I wouldn't mind having my faults recognized, too. I would like it to be said that I was always willing to help in whatever way I could for whomever I could — but come against me and mine, and I will turn into a one-woman guerilla warfare team.

In my lifetime, I have been told that I was kind, beautiful inside and out, polite, helpful, passionate, talented, determined, intelligent, stubborn, independent but needful, loving, funny, expressive, devoted, emotional, deserving, commanding, powerful and strong willed. It would be an honor to still be described in any or all of those ways in my winter years.

I would like, on my 80th birthday to have more than one person say that I am a grand old dame, full of piss and vinegar, with humor in my heart and voice to invoke laughter every day from my friends, family or strangers with whom I strike up conversations. Someone should say I have a heart full of love and am willing to take others to my heart for healing, that I would offer food, a shoulder to cry on and an ear to listen with.

The most important words to hear on that most auspicious of days would be: "Happy Birthday, lady, and many more. Remember, you are not getting older, just getting better. I love you!"

By Derek Flynn

WHAT DO I WANT PEOPLE TO SAY about me on my 80th birthday? I don't think there are too many people who would say: "Well, on my 80th birthday, I would hope they'll be reading out my list of charges at the War Crimes Tribunal." No, the fact is we all want the same thing: As we reach our twilight years, we hope that people will say, "He was a good person. He was talented. He touched many people. He was loved and he loved in return." But no matter what we hope for, there is no guarantee that everybody is going to say this about us at the end of our lives.

Take the example of writer Christopher Hitchens, who died recently at the age of 62. Immediately after his death, all the great and good, such as Martin Amis, Stephen Fry and Salman Rushdie, gathered to eulogize him. If you were to read what they wrote about him, you would think Hitchens was one of the greatest men who ever lived, but there were just as many people who came out not to praise him but to bury him. If you listened to the detractors, you would think Hitchens was the devil incarnate. The fact is he was neither; he was just a person, the same as anyone else. Besides, even saints don't get a completely free ride at the end of their lives. Even Mother Teresa had her critics. Indeed, Hitchens himself wrote disparagingly of her after her death.

So, what would I like people to say about me at my 80th birthday? All the above-mentioned statements, of course. But I have no control over what people say. No matter how I live my life, no matter how much of a good life I think I've led, no matter how well I think I've treated people, there may always be someone who doesn't see it that way.

I've always admired Henry Miller, author of the once-banned novel *Tropic of Cancer* (amongst many others). And while I'm a huge fan of that book, it's not Miller's books that I admire so much as his life. He lived his life in various acts, so to speak. Born in 1891 on the cusp of the 20th century, his first act was growing up in Brooklyn, getting married and struggling to make ends meet. The second act started in 1930, when Miller was 39 and moved to Paris. He spent 10 years there, penniless for most of it. It was there that Henry Miller the struggling writer became Henry Miller the artist. Paris was where he completed or began most of his major works. It was also where he had many of the encounters that would make up the mythos of Henry Miller, such as his affair with Anais Nin.

Miller left Paris at the outbreak of World War II and moved back to America, eventually settling in Big Sur, Calif. This began the next act of his life. In 1961, the ban on *Tropic of Cancer* was lifted and, as time went on and the book became widely available, Miller became something of a counter-culture icon to the hippies of the 1960s. You would think this would have been the swansong of his life, as he was now in his 70s, but he lived for another two decades, eventually dying in 1980 at the ripe old age of 89.

It's extraordinary to think of the things Miller saw from 1891 to 1980, the changes that took place in the world around him. That's certainly one of the things I would like people to say on my 80th birthday, that I'd lived long enough to see extraordinary changes in the world. And perhaps that I, too, lived my life in different acts. Miller, having lived his life in so many acts, met a variety of people. And those who remembered him, remembered him sometimes very differently. Some of his ex-wives and ex-lovers remembered him with fondness; others were not so kind. Some of his friends took umbrage at the way he portrayed them in his books; others simply laughed it off. Some thought of him as a charming, witty and gregarious friend; others saw him as someone who was on the make, always on the lookout for a free meal or a free bed (and, indeed, someone to share that bed with).

The fact is he was probably all of these things. We are never that *one* person throughout our lives. Indeed, we are never that one person at *any* one point in our lives. We have different faces for different people. That's just how life is. Our co-workers may not see the same face our loved ones see, and so on. If you're a performer, you get up in front of a crowd wearing a face that's not necessarily your "true" face but a different aspect of you. So it's a simple fact that everyone is going to remember us differently. And all we can hope for when we sit down to blow out those 80 candles is that however people remember us they do it with a glint in their eye.

WRITE FOR THE FIGHT

By Jesse James Freeman

THE NIGHT BEFORE MY 80TH BIRTHDAY, I will have passed.

Having a conversation about yourself after you're dead — it's a very film-noir approach to looking at the end of a life. Nothing you say at that point should really matter anymore, should it? The die is cast, and the Wicked Witch's hourglass has let the sand run down. Adventure time in mortal-coil land is over, if we are to consider time in the linear sense. You're now out of hit-points; the story has ended. Your journey is bankrupt, and the debt must be paid. The only things left are the flashbacks.

I have never considered that I would be long lived. The concept that I would even make it to 80 is alien to me. I have taken chances, many of which, at best, were ill advised. I have put more years on this already ancient-feeling body than could ever be good for it. I felt like I was 50 when I was about 10 years old. I guess you could consider me to be an old soul. In my 20s, I was already yelling at kids to get off my lawn — although I did mask my old-man nature pretty well with all the partying I did in Hollywood during that time.

I never got too lost in it, this life. Like the characters I write about in my silly adventure novels, I always had "a mission," a greater cause that allowed me to press on and kept me grounded (to an extent). I should have gotten into a lot more trouble than I did during this life, but I always knew better. I always had goals in place, and the excessive drinking, hell raising and cavalier attitude acted as an unstoppable force as I skated across that rail of time.

Time is linear from a human's perspective, and our thinking only disengages from this truth when we become obsessed with the "what came before" of our past or the "what could become" of our future. To live in these imaginary worlds is where we are prone to err the most. Yes, I said it: Even the past is an imaginary world. True enough to our perception, all those things happened, but what makes the past a dream is when we remain attached to it and refuse to leave it where it belongs, far behind us.

Sometimes we live in the past, thinking we can change it. We keep our finger on the rewind button and keep remixing that tape over and over in our heads. Other times, we fast forward to the future and dream of what might be if everything in the universe lines up just right.

We lose ourselves to memories of things that didn't happen as we wished they had and to thoughts of things that will never be. In doing so, we ignore the only point of the equation that will ever matter. How are we this very second? What am I doing that means anything to me and to anyone who happens to be right next to me? Am I being true to myself and to those I keep so very close to my heart?

On my 80th birthday, sadly I am no more. What do I hope people will say about me? I hope they say that in the moments we were together that I lived in the moment and took so very little for granted. I hope they say that when I loved, I loved completely, and when I hated, I let it all out and then moved past it. I hope they say I made them laugh. I hope they tell stories about me at my own expense and that this, too, makes them laugh — because if you can't make fun of me when I'm dead, well...

But I hope they don't dwell on any of it too much, because most of all I would never want them to lose sight of all the fantastic things they still have left to do in their present.

By Laura Kilmartin

THERE IS A WORLD OF DIFFERENCE between what I would like people to say about me on my 80th birthday and what they might actually say.

In my shameful heart of hearts, I would most like to hear, "Wow. I never thought I'd see a woman that age rock a pair of leather pants like that. You go, grandma!"

I am not proud, but while we're at it, I suppose it would also be incredibly satisfying to overhear a conversation that begins, "Isn't it lovely how modest she is, despite her vast fortune?"

Finally, if I am truly being honest, I could die a happy woman if, on my 80th birthday, someone were to comment: "She and husband George Clooney have never looked more in love."

While I do not expect these statements will ever be made about me, I hope others do not judge me too harshly for the dream. Besides, I defy any woman to take a deep look inward and tell me that my list is far removed from her own. Everyone has a shallow streak within — if we really look for it. It is found in the same area of the brain responsible for driving us to stalk our ex-boyfriends on Facebook.

If I admit that thin thighs, Rockefeller wealth and a Hollywood romance may not be realistic, then what do I want people to say about me on my 80th birthday?

More than anything, I want them to say, "She's the one I call when..." It doesn't matter how they finish the sentence, because the content of the message is not nearly as important as the fact that they call.

I would like to be thought of as the person my friends call on when they want to share a laugh, cry a few tears or jump in the car for an impromptu weekend at the beach. I have had the good fortune to be cast in the role of travel companion, empathetic listener and the Ethel to more than one Lucy during my first 40 years on this planet. To spend the next 40 years the same way — called upon as a partner in crime when people find themselves navigating the sometimes rough but always thrilling rapids of daily life — would be a great gift.

I have been lucky enough to check a number of items off my bucket list. I have climbed a mountain in Scotland, ridden horses in Texas and snorkeled off the coast of Mexico. I danced in the aisles while Springsteen played to thousands in Fenway Park and heard Gregory Peck tell the stories of his life from a small, intimate stage. While I have embarked on these somewhat grand adventures, I have also derived great pleasure from playing with my nephews in my parents' backyard pool and listening to a friend strum his guitar for a few dozen patrons in the back room of a seedy bar.

The formula I followed to create so many wonderful memories and experiences is very simple: When my friends called and offered me an opportunity, I accepted it. Limited only by those pesky details of time and money, I showed up to the dance and tried to fill every slot on my card with every vacation, movie date and poetry slam that came my way.

Wanting to be the person my friends call on is not always about fun and adventure, though. There have been times when I was the one to get the call that something horrible had happened, leaving me as the top branch of the phone tree responsible for making my own calls to rally the troops. I have listened to people I love cry, knowing I could offer no solution to ease their pain. In times of need, I have been asked by friends to care for children, pets and — on one occasion — a hosta bush.

I have been very fortunate, though, that for every call I answered to hold a hand in heartbreak, I have answered dozens more to lift a glass aloft in celebration. For every wake I have attended, there have been even more christenings. For every dull evening spent wishing I had stayed home in my pajamas watching *Laverne & Shirley* reruns, there have been hundreds of nights like the recent one spent at the Wolf's Den at Mohegan Sun casino, enraptured by Christian Kane singing the virtues of country women.

When I am sitting at my 80th birthday party listening to my friends talk about me, I want to hear someone say, "I'll give you a call tomorrow so we can..."

Whether that sentence ends with "rent motorcycles and drive up the coast," "pick up tickets to the theater" or "sit quietly and talk," will not matter to me. I will simply answer the call.

By Marni Mann

MY DAUGHTER'S EYES ARE A REPLICA of my own — just less aged and more vibrant. The expression on her face shows me she's the woman I taught her to be: confident, educated and motherly. My achievements have afforded her every opportunity; she took each one and excelled to the best of her ability. Her children are mature and intelligent — just like their parents — and each one has tapped into their respective talents and begun a promising career.

My son's teeth gleam in the overhead light. His smile is wide and excited; it matches my personality. He's inherited my charisma — how to dazzle his listeners with different gestures — but he relies on his smarts to charm. Determined and goal oriented in his work ethic — just like me — he has become a successful man and doting grandfather. His kids are beautiful, like-minded to their parents, respectful and cultured.

When I was raising my children, they didn't always accept the scholarly nudges I gave, and they often challenged my lectures about perseverance. My husband, who pushed our children just as hard toward greatness, praised my determination and believed it contributed to my triumphs. He understood how career oriented I was, but my career often took me away from my family. I was fortunate to have a partner who supported my passion and commitment; he filled in as both a mother and father when I wasn't present. And now, as my life draws near its close, I find myself revisiting what I could have improved on when it came to being a mother and a wife, contemplating how much time I spent on my career and how my dominating personality could have been perceived.

My son and daughter show me how proud they are to have me as their mother. They recognize the sacrifices and responsibilities that come with parenting — and they acknowledge them. My children appreciate what I was able to offer them emotionally and financially, and they have used those advantages to become better people, positive role models, influencers for good, professional leaders and outstanding parents and grandparents. My children and grandchildren so closely resemble my husband and me. Even though we often questioned our choices as parents, we must have done something right.

I wasn't born to only be inspired by the darker side of life — though I am an author of dark fiction — or to create stories just in my head. My purpose has been to translate these thoughts and ideas onto the page. My work has been acknowledged not simply because my novels were published but because my words made a difference. My books have entertained, triggered emotions and changed the views of readers. My first novel, a story about addiction, brought about awareness of the issue, taught the families and friends of an addict how to stop enabling, and changed opinions about addiction being a disease and not a choice. I do not measure my success by book sales but by the responses from my readers. They've shared with me their smiles, tears and bouts of laughter. They've told me how they relate to aspects of each story, and they've expressed a desire to share my titles with their friends and family members.

The people I've encountered have touched my life; in the process, I've been able to touch their lives in return. I've helped people locate their creative side and inner genius, and my words have affected them in a positive way. My sense of hope drifted into their soul, and they've been able to achieve their own personal success. I've lived by the motto of paying it forward and giving back; these practices have proven worthy. Assisting others and doing good deeds brings about powerful results.

In my 80 years, I've had the opportunity to meet many survivors — and they've shared their stories with me. The tragedies they've overcome vary in degree. One person's experience isn't easier, more difficult or more challenging than someone else's, their experiences are just different. We all have scars, whether they're hidden beneath our skin or visual to the eye. I view my scars as battle wounds; they are testament to the struggles I've endured. Some experiences went horribly wrong, and painful memories have left their brand. But with each one, I came out victorious. I survived. At my 80th birthday party, they call me a survivor.

By Karla J. Nellenbach

A *"Breaking News"* bulletin flashes across the screen just seconds before the camera zeroes in on the neatly coiffed anchorwoman stationed behind the news desk

The anchorwoman clears her throat dramatically.

"We've just learned that, Karla Nellenbach — famed adventurer, zombie hunter, unicorn wrangler and current world-record holder for most consecutive terms served as president of the Mr. T fan club — has passed away."

There's a pause as the camera flips to show the infamous photo of Karla standing atop a mound of freshly slaughtered undead, holding up the head of the general of the zombie army, Abraham Lincoln.

"Known throughout the world for her many philanthropic contributions, Nellenbach was most recognized for her role in ending the last zombie apocalypse nearly 40 years ago. Before that event, it was believed that only a bullet shot directly into the brain could kill a zombie. But that last uprising of the undead gave birth to a new mutant variety of zombie, and the bullets no longer worked. It wasn't until the explosion heard round the world that the new weapon was discovered."

"Holed up in her house with her two dogs, ammo dwindling and the horde that surrounded her multiplying by the second, Nellenbach made what she called a last-ditch attempt at fighting off the zombies by using a concoction that closely resembled homemade napalm. It was composed of equal parts gasoline and orange juice. Later, she credited the soap-making scene from the movie *Fight Club* as leading to her success in ridding the world of the walking dead."

The camera returns to the anchorwoman as she shuffles papers before staring headlong into the lens.

"Since then, May 24th, Nellenbach's birthday, has been recognized as a worldwide day of celebration and independence. Each

153

year, her birthday bash has been bigger and more raucous than the last. As this was her 80th year on Earth, her family had decided to promote her many accomplishments over the years with a costume-themed extravaganza."

Earlier taped footage floods the screen as viewers are treated to a parade of garishly costumed movie stars, politicians, business tycoons and other noted celebrities.

"As you can see, many of Nellenbach's admirers chose to attend the evening's festivities sporting muscle shirts, Mohawks and heavy gold jewelry while others donned unicorn costumes. But the most popular disguise of the evening was that of the zombie, complete with ripped, bloodstained clothing and ghostly pale skin. This, we believe, is where the night went terribly wrong. For more on this breaking story, we go live in the field to correspondent, Mike Hadfield. Mike?"

The screen cuts to live feed of a stone-faced gentleman staring gravely into the camera. Behind him, the decimated, still-burning ruins of a once glorious mansion lay crumbling. Police and emergency service personnel climb through the wreckage, searching for any form of life.

"It's a grim scene here, Tammy," he begins. "What began as a night of great celebration has ended in flames and a death toll well into the hundreds. Right now, details are sketchy, but Karla Nellenbach and her family are presumed dead."

"Do we know what could have possibly caused this explosion?" Tammy's voice cuts in.

Slowly, reluctantly, the on-scene reporter nods.

"Well, Tammy, you may recall that early last year, Nellenbach was diagnosed with a rare, extremely aggressive form of brain cancer. The doctors believe that her days of hunting unicorns in the wilds of Tibet coupled with the sheer amount of toxic exposure to her homemade napalm — which eventually eradicated all of zombie kind — contributed to the lesions on her brain. They had given her only a few months to live, but, of course, the tough old broad famously declared that she didn't plan on dying before her 80th birthday."

154

The reporter pauses, glancing over his shoulder at the wreckage. "According to sources close to the adventurer's family, Nellenbach's mental state has been slowly declining in the last several weeks, causing her to experience vivid hallucinations in which she's relived many of her past exploits. Unfortunately for her guests tonight, the zombie costumes threw her into one such episode."

"Oh, my!" Tammy exclaims. "What happened?"

"Well, Tammy, it appears that upon seeing her family and friends turned into the walking dead, Nellenbach, still spry and faster in her walker than her 16-year-old grandson, hightailed it to the state-of-the-art panic room in her basement — which was reportedly stocked with enough napalm to blow the entire North American continent off the map. She proceeded to lock herself in, and before her husband or children could get to her to explain what was going on, she'd armed two of the bombs in her bunker, and, well..." he trails off, again shooting a look over his shoulder.

The reporter clears his throat and faces the camera once more.

"One lucky survivor, however, claims to have heard Nellenbach shouting through the home's intercom system," the reporter says, looking down at the note card in his hand. "I quote, 'You'll never *expletive* take me alive you *expletive* undead bastards ...' end quote."

The screen flips back to Tammy at the anchor desk.

"Well," she says after a dazed minute. "There you have it. Confirmed reports of famed zombie hunter Karla Nellenbach being taken down earlier tonight after she mistakenly believed another zombie apocalypse was on the horizon. For more on this horrific tragedy, tune in to our coverage at 11, when we will take an in-depth look at a long, celebrated life that ended in senseless violence and tragedy."

Screen fades out and goes to a commercial featuring a much younger, more mentally stable Karla, who is grinning while drinking a Dr. Pepper, the official soft drink of zombie hunters everywhere.

By Terry Persun

I READ A LONG TIME AGO that there are worse things to be than kind. At 80, I'd like to be thought of as kind. Regardless of whether I wrote a great novel, excelled at playing an instrument or created a corporation, kindness is the one attribute that can go with anything I choose to do.

This doesn't mean that I haven't done things that I'm not proud of or that I've never hurt someone's feelings. What it means is that I always had the best intentions, whether it was doing what I thought was right at the time or telling the truth when it needed to be said. Kindness has to do with what you intend, not what others perceive.

If I were to prioritize from this one point, then perhaps the question I'd much rather answer isn't what people might say about me when I reach a ripe old age but what might I think about myself. Specifically, I want to know that I didn't give up on what was important to me, that I fed my soul every day of my life, and that I was happier and healthier because of it. I want to know that I did my best, that I didn't cheat or lie to *get* something but rather that I did the right thing to *achieve* it.

When I'm 80, there's got to be room for me to continue exploring myself, my art and my beliefs. I'd like to be open to new ideas and thoughts, and new ways of doing things or looking at the world. An old acquaintance once said about me that I was always "pissed off and raising hell." It wasn't until later that a counselor suggested that I wasn't pissed off but passionate. I love that idea. And I wasn't so much a hell-raiser as a rebellious and independent thinker. Now we're talking. I'd like people to know that I loved life and lived it full throttle, pedal to the metal.

If I live to be 80, I hope to feel as though I raised hell enough to satisfy my personality and explored my passions without regret. That I loved the best that I could every day, day after day. Frank Sinatra sang it well: "I did it my way." Who could dispute that kind of life? As much as it would be nice to have others say great things about me when I'm 80, I'm going to be happy if I do my self-evaluation and come out satisfied with where I am at the time and that I enjoyed the trip getting there.

I write to focus my passion so that others might learn to be equally independent in the ways they think. I wish everyone on the planet understood that they are allowed to make a decision just because they want to. So many people seem to feel as though they need an excuse for everything they think and do. Sometimes, you get to say, "Because I wanted to," with no reasons attached to it other than that.

In a world where so many people are bent on gaining something in order to remain ahead of the game or being something primarily for appearances, it would be great if we'd all just accept who we are without excuses. Believe in yourself and what you choose to do. It's not about money; it's about passion and love and kindness. And raising a little hell. Before you care about what others have to say, ask yourself this question: Have you taken the time to do the things you love to do?

As I get older, I notice that my filters fall away. This is a good thing. As I get closer and closer to a ripe old age, I hope I get more honest with myself (and others). I hope that I make choices based on what I want, not what I think I should want. I hope to do what pleases me, not what pleases everyone around me.

I'm trying to do these things now and — despite my passionate and independent spirit — still find that I hedge in the direction of acceptance more often than I'd like. By the time I'm 80, I hope I can look back and say that I seldom compromised, that I was honest and passionate about life. I want to feel as though I was always kind. And that I never gave up.

By Laura Tiberio

WHEN I AM 80 YEARS OLD, the only raised voices coming from my house will belong to my great-grandchildren, shrieking with delight as I give them tissue-paper kisses. The only things of value in my house will be the books I have read, pictures I have taken and memories I have made. Knickknacks will be treasured only if crafted by the hands of those younger than 11 years.

When I am 80, and my hair is fine and white, I hope my copper dolphin clip will still hold it tight. I hope my rings still slide past my knuckles and I can still paint my own toes. When I go out, I will wear what I like — perhaps Doc Martens with fishnets and my wool peacoat over the lot. I will not wear pantsuits or cut my hair short and sleep in curlers, nor will I use White Shoulders perfume. Those things are for old people!

When I am 80, I will play music on whatever contraption made sense to me when I last cared to keep up with technology. I will play it loud and often. And I will dance around my kitchen, should my legs still allow it, and wheel myself up and down the hall if they should not. I will watch the sun rise every morning, eager for another race across the sky. Though I may not be nimble enough to keep pace or have the stamina to sit out all day, I will still enjoy the golden rays the sun casts on my window, warming my face as it passes.

When I am 80, I will remember my youth, how exhilarating it was to have so many years out in front with so much anticipation and how the burdens of reality did not yet weigh me down. But I will also remember my middle age and how burdens became blessings under the hammer of perspective.

When I am 80, my family will still be close to me, even if they have moved far away. I shall outlive some friends but keep making new ones. I will still matter in the hearts and minds of others; I pray I still have the wits to matter to myself. Of course, I don't really know ... yet.

WINTER

When I am 80, what will be the chatter as I pass by? Will it be funny to them, my shuffle-step? Will they murmur about my dated clothes? Will they be patient with me as I fumble with my pocketbook, spilling change on the counter to pay for my dinner? When I am 80, will "old" be all they are able to see?

When I am 80, I want to be generous with smiles and stingy with advice. I want talk of literature to prevail over talk of rheumatism, sunset walks to have precedence over evening news, and a stranger to see my eyes sparkle and long to become a friend. Because when I am 80, I hope my life will have produced a spirit strong and spry enough to proudly carry a body in decline.

When I am 80 years old, this is what I hope others will say:

"Look there. See that house? All those cars, all those travelers? That's my neighbor, celebrating her 80th birthday today. Oh, man, she bakes the best pumpkin bread; I can smell it every Wednesday morning. Always brings me a piece when I'm out walking my dog. Let's go over and wish her well."

"Mom wanted to make lasagna for the party, but we told her she couldn't cook her own birthday dinner! She fussed a bit until we agreed to let her make the cake. She taught everyone in the family how to cook — particularly buttermilk pancakes, sauce and spice cookies. You couldn't move out until you had perfected those things. Of course, we had mastered them by the time we were 3. But her cakes ... no one can make 'em quite right — except Mom."

"Growing up she took on all sorts of amazing adventures: ice skating, movies, swimming, museums, plays. Remember those summers she took us camping all by herself, even when everyone said she was crazy? Just packed the car and away we went!"

"Grandma is the best storyteller. She can make up stuff right in her very own head while she is talking to us! And when she reads, she does all the voices. Her voice gets really soft when it's scary or sad and then really loud when it's exciting! Oh, and she has all these old paper books on the shelf in her study. Some she even wrote herself and someone printed them!"

"Took me into her home, gave me a place to stay when I needed somewhere to go. Always felt like a part of the family."

159

"Her house is like the center of the universe; it has this pull that just draws you. When you are here, be it just in the kitchen with a cup of tea or enjoying dinner with a crowd, she makes you feel welcome and at home."

"The door is always open. My kids spent a good portion of their elementary years doing laps through her kitchen."

"With her there is no pretense, no awkward manner and no need for constant small talk. It's so easy to just relax and have a good time."

"She has always been there for me. And whenever I felt overwhelmed or just needed to vent, all I had to do was call. Maybe she had to holler at the kids a few times during the phone conversation, but she would always make sure I was okay before she hung up."

"Very respected in her field. Her work touched thousands of families."

"Her smile still lights me up — just like when I was a little kid. I look in her eyes, and I still see her endless, unwavering support. It lets me know that anything I truly want and work hard for is within my reach."

"What a firecracker. Such spirit, I hope I have that much energy when I reach her age."

"Hey, Dad, you still enchanted with Mom?" Response: "Something like that!"

"Hey, you all, it's Laura's birthday. Cut the chatter! Break out the wine, turn down the lights and crank up the music. Let's get this party started!"

When I am 80, I hope I am remembered well — but I am not really worried.

I will spend all 80 years making sure I am not forgotten.

By Laura Zera

"HELLFIRE AND DAMNATION. IS THAT WOMAN the only person here to whom the laws of gravity do not apply?"

It's going to be a roof-raising shindig (my 80th birthday party), and attendees will utter such exclamations as I blithely cha-cha across the dance floor with my husband of 46 years. (Although handsome, he's not a strong lead and is lacking in grace and coordination. All of that is secondary, though, as his main job as my dance partner is to show me off).

Many of us are now a wee bit on the deaf side, so for the partygoers who want to stand up and make toasts and comments during the dinner portion of the program, there will be a microphone on the podium. And a booster step. We've also shrunk.

"I've known some of these people for 65 years!" I'll yell at my husband. And while I will blush and frequently raise my hand to my mouth in modesty while people regale us with stories, truly I am basking in all of the glorious attention. Even at 80, I like to feel like a princess for a day.

There are some things people *won't* be able to say about me. No one can call me a dedicated and outstanding mother, as I never had children. That rules out adoring grandmother, too. Anything complimentary to do with food preparation is off the list, as are singing, snapping my fingers or consistency in sending out Christmas cards and remembering important dates.

My husband will tell everyone that I am a loving and wonderful wife, even though I still nag him about spending too much money on olives and stinky cheese. My sister and nephews will say they love me dearly despite the fact that I give them gifts of Kim Jong Il tongue scrapers, adhesive mustache kits and other such things. We will all hug, because I'm a hugger. And then what? What other words do I most want to hear from the people who have come to share this day with me?

"Laura Zera is a true and loyal friend." It's a simple proclamation, but it would confirm for me that my deep want for meaningful connection with other human beings has been recognized and appreciated. A wise woman recently said to me, "I collect people." *I do, too!* I thought. My heart is like a map, except the permanent pushpins aren't for all the places that I've been; they are for the people who affected me along the way.

I worry about this proclamation, though, and whether these and other similar words will form in the mouths of my cronies and chums when I become an octogenarian. I moved away from my longtime friends when I got married and then devoted more time to creating something special with my partner (followed closely by house chores and other mundane tasks) than to outings with new friends in our chosen hometown. Good friendships will adjust to fit, yes, but in a tussle between "absence makes the heart grow fonder" and "out of sight, out of mind," I would still put my five-spot on the latter. Friendships are not cacti; they take a bit of work.

Life has that habit of moving by so quickly; like the water in a river after a spell of heavy rain, it has its own current. Months become years and years become decades. All of the phone numbers that were programmed in my memory have washed away, eroded by disuse. My head is left brimming with unfulfilled intentions to call and check in with my friends. The reality is my actions don't show them nearly enough how much they mean to me.

This must change, I have realized. I can't wait until I'm 80 to find out how deeply this true-and-loyal-friend business has manifested! I want people to say it on my 50th birthday — and my 60th. I want them to say it tomorrow. I must be that person *now*. It's time to dig out some stamps and make use of that unlimited long-distance calling plan. The dang laundry can wait.

There are yet other things that I want people to say about me, both now and later: that I'm positive and supportive, resilient and courageous, inspiring and kind. I want them to say that I have lived fearlessly (although I will know there was lots of fear; I just hid it well). It would fill me with honor to hear that my writing has had an effect on people, that it made them think differently about the world and aspire to be more positive, supportive, resilient, courageous, inspiring and kind.

These are some of the things I want to be part of my *living legacy*. Different from the traditional sense of the word, my life's legacy is more important than leaving a gift of property or money when I depart this earth. It's where I find my thoughts lingering after vanity and ego give way to the weightier subject of how to make a positive impact before I leave (she says to herself while studiously applying face cream every night).

I'm learning to design my living legacy by paying attention to how I incorporate my gifts and values in the way I live my life every single day. I endeavor to focus on the intention behind my actions and the level of mindfulness that I bring to everything I do. It's about being as purposeful as possible throughout all of my years, so that when I get to 80, people aren't just saying great things about me because they've had two glasses of wine at the party and can't hold their liquor the way they used to. They'll be saying it because I lived in a way that made a difference — to them, to my community and to the world. And that's what I *really* want. Cha-cha-cha!

By Tracey M. Hansen, Co-Author

RANDOM RELATIVE STANDS UP to give a heartfelt speech. This person is young and hot and has obviously inherited all of my genes.*
"We are here to celebrate Tracey turning 80 years young. She couldn't be here today because of a prior commitment to shoot the December cover of *Playboy*, but she gave me something to read to all of you on her behalf."

* * *

To the thousands of you who are gathered today to celebrate me:
I don't trust any of you to properly honor my 80th birthday, so here are a few things I want you to be thinking about on this most grand occasion.
I have made many wonderful decisions in my 80 years on this planet. For example, it was a great decision on my part to have entire-body Botox injections every day since turning 30, thus keeping me better looking than all of you. After turning down Prince Harry's proposal and marrying the love of my life, ManPal, I have never regretted the decision to grow our three children in Petri dishes — as opposed to letting the little bastards destroy what God (and science) have made perfect.
The proudest moments of my life, thus far, have been:
- Winning the Pulitzer (which they now call The Tracey Award)
- Those 10 years hunting alligators in the bayou
- Discovering how to alter alcohol to make it healthy
- The eight years I spent in the White House alongside Vice President Bieber
- Implementing National No Pants Thursdays
- Taking up a British accent
- Leading the great World War IV victory over the Kardashians
- Winning the sixth grade Language Arts award
- Answering 11 questions correctly in a single episode of Jeopardy

WINTER

- And the time Meryl Streep gave me the stink-eye at that charity art auction

I know I've spent the majority of the last 80 years fairly drunk; therefore, I may not remember most of your names — except, of course, for my three beautiful children: Riesling, Merlot and Cabernet. And just because I do not know what the fuck your name is doesn't mean that I don't love (or at least possess some minute affection for) each and every one of you. My only hope is that when you look in the mirror at your stunning blue eyes and well-developed calf muscles that you are grateful to me that you are not ugly as fuck.

I am glad I never took life too seriously. Pantsing my children and husband in public was (and still is) one of my favorite activities — as are beer-pong and speed texting.

I have purchased an additional 80 years through NASA's life-expansion program and will outlive all of you. But on the off chance one of you squeaks by the 160-year mark, just remember when I die that my body is to be turned over to the scientists I keep locked up housed in my basement. They have instructions to store my severed head in a freezer until a time when it can be thawed and reattached to the body of a primate. Also, when I am long gone, there is a small disk in my safe-deposit box at the bank that should be turned over to the CIA. At that time, it would be wise for some of you to take on alternative identities, because I may or may not have implicated you in several high-profile, um, shall we say, incidents.

Although I was not able to make it today, I do have several spies in your midst. So, let me just say that my party had better be more elaborate than a cheese tray and a box of wine. If this is the case, my spies will be handing out red slips that detail your disinheritance. (Although there may not be much to inherit considering I just purchased a hovercraft and spent millions having it bedazzled with pink Swarovski crystals.) If your gift to me on this momentous occasion consists of any sort of gift card, you will be led out by security to an undisclosed location where you will be forced to watch circa 2009 reruns of *Saturday Night Live* — otherwise known as the dark age of television.

I hope all of you who have given me wonderful gifts have a wonderful time at my party. I don't know when I will see you all again, but I will have my secretary forward my schedule so that you will know where I am and what fabulous things I am doing. I will leave you with this final thought: After 80 years of living with a childish enthusiasm for life, I regret absolutely nothing. (Except the great absinthe incident of 2020, which you can read all about on my Wikipedia page.)

Word to your mother.

CONCLUSION

Conclusion –Some Closing Thoughts
By Tracey M. Hansen, co-author

When Tess Hardwick asked me to be her partner for this anthology, I was both flattered and confused. Why me? I'm just a foul-mouthed blogger who recently wrote about what women think while watching porn, and she is a brilliant author with a best-selling Nook book. Then she explained her idea to me, and I had one of those slap-my-own-forehead moments where I thought, *"Why didn't I think of that?"* With our contrasting voices and unique styles, Tess and I were meant to be partners on a book that focuses on our differences. She helped me to realize that it doesn't matter what walk of life we come from, what our goals are, where we live or how much money we have, we all have been affected by cancer or know someone who has.

I am going to be honest. I use humor as a shield. It protects me from people knowing who I really am or what I am really about. So, I hope you can forgive me for not being funny, just for a minute, so I can best explain to you my personal thoughts on this disease.

I've written this conclusion about a million times, all with jokes and swear words, all the while thinking about my wonderful Uncle Gary. We lost him this past April to brain cancer. At only 50 years old, and a year after his diagnosis, he left behind two bright college-age boys and my brave, beautiful aunt, who is now forced to re-evaluate her place in this world without the person she expected to grow old with. I was a flower girl at their wedding. He let me dance on his feet and never complained about the annoying 4-year-old who wouldn't let him leave the dance floor. When I gave a reading at his service, I didn't think of the words I was saying but rather the family he was leaving behind. Where does all the love go when someone who was so immensely loved is no longer here?

Uncle Gary may not have been battling breast cancer, but cancer in any of its forms should no longer be allowed to crash into our lives and leave us tangled and twisted in its wreckage. My Aunt Janine should not be going through her second bout with the disease, my mom shouldn't have to get slices dug out of her skin and muscle because of malignant melanoma, and my Aunt Christine should not have to plan her future without my Uncle Gary.

At just 28 years old, a former Miss Venezuela recently lost her life to breast cancer, leaving behind a 2-year-old daughter. Don't wait to get your mammograms. Screw the recommended age of 40 to wait until your first one. Breast cancer doesn't check IDs at the door. And it doesn't care if your ta-ta's are homegrown or store bought. So make that appointment today. If you're feeling feisty, write a letter to your congressman and tell them that breast cancer has no age but it has many faces, some of which you have known and lost.

The authors in this anthology have graciously dedicated their talents and time to help us donate money to abolish this disease. All author proceeds will be given to help fund cancer research. Each book sold will help to prevent more families from being torn apart at the seams. By purchasing this book and encouraging others to buy it, you have made a difference. From the bottoms of our hearts, we thank you. I couldn't have asked for a better collaborator than the brilliant and inspirational Tess Hardwick or a better publishing team than Heather Ludviksson and Katherine Sears at Booktrope Publishing. A sincere thank you to all of the charities that work to keep families whole by funding research that will, we hope, one day leave future generations to ask their elders, "What exactly *was* cancer?"

Just like the four seasons of the year, the seasons of our lives are ever changing. No matter what we do, we cannot prevent the world around us from moving. Even if we stand perfectly still, we can still feel the cold bite of winter or the hot sun of summer against our skin. Changes cannot be avoided. We have all been 5, most of you have been 20, we all have life goals, and I hope that we will all reach that 80th birthday. So, my advice to you is this: Don't stand still. Move within and around this beautiful life you have been given and, someday, if you are fortunate enough — well after that 80th birthday

CONCLUSION

— you will leave this world behind with your close friends and family members wondering what to do with all the love they had for you.
—WTYM

Contributors

Gordon Bonnet

Gordon Bonnet has been writing with great enthusiasm ever since his first story, *Crazy Bird Bends His Beak,* won critical acclaim in Mrs. Moore's first grade class at Central Elementary School in St. Albans, W.Va. His more recent works usually have to do with the realm of the paranormal, although frequent excursions into the world of the past betray his fascination with history.

When he's not writing, Gordon can be most often found teaching high school biology or playing the flute in contra-dance bands in and around Ithaca, N.Y. He also plays the bagpipes (but would prefer if you'd keep that hush-hush).

Galit Breen

Once upon a time, Galit Breen was a TRAVELER. She met amazing people and ate delicious food. All was well with her world. Then she started her real life. She became a STUDENT, earning a B.S. in human development and an M.A. in education. She became a classroom and reading TEACHER. She met a man on the Internet (when it was still *gasp*-worthy and new) and became his WIFE. Shortly after that, she became a MINNESOTAN. (He still owes her one for that.) But the biggest earthquake shake to Galit's soul was becoming a MOM. The interrupted sleep, the crying, the diapers. But there was also the attachment, the touch, the bungee cords to her heart. Today her labels are woven together. Tightly. *A wife of one! A mama of three! And a brand-new puggle owner!* To keep her grounded and to offset the lack of sleep, Galit writes. An accomplished essayist, she has work scheduled for publication in forthcoming anthologies about motherhood, marriage and faith. Galit is currently writing her first novel and blogs at TheseLittleWaves.com

F. Jo Bruce

Once upon a time, F. Jo's first-grade teacher instilled in her a love of phonics, words and reading. Her fifth-grade teacher was the first to comment on F. Jo's love of creating the written word, followed later by acknowledgements from her eighth-grade teacher and a pair of English instructors in high school. Decades after being in her class, F. Jo encountered her eighth-grade teacher, who asked F. Jo if she was still writing. She replied , "I was, I am, I do."

Drawing not only from her own personal life experiences but also from those of anyone willing to share, F. Jo's chosen genre is short stories and memoirs. Her dad was a storyteller, and F. Jo absorbed his tales. Harboring his stories and those of which she has personal knowledge, she remembers and treasures the tales of her past. There are whole books in her brain, but the short story light shines brightest at this time in her life.

F. Jo and her husband live in the foothills of the Ozark Mountains on their 5-acre "homestead" with three dogs. Returning to the basics of living, they live in a one-room cabin with solar power, a composting toilet and no running water (yet). It's hard work, and sometimes overwhelming, but F. Jo finds the rewards make it all worthwhile. The work never ends; every day brings something new. She describes their lives as simplistic but comfortable and satisfying.

A passion for natural healing keeps F. Jo busy learning and studying about the uses of herbs and plants. An herbalist is just one of the things she would like to be when she "grows up." Written words are F. Jo's friends; through them she finds expression, comfort, joy, fodder and a way to give to others. For them and what they bring, she is forever thankful and blessed.

Derek Flynn

Derek Flynn is an Irish musician and writer who resides in Waterford, Ireland. Derek's work has been published in *The Irish Times*, and he was also first runner-up for the 2011 J. G. Farrell Award for Best Novel-In-Progress. His writing/music blog, titled "Rant, with Occasional Music," can be found at <u>derekflynn.wordpress.com</u>. You can find and follow Derek on Twitter at <u>twitter.com/ - !/derekf03</u>.

Jesse James Freeman

Jesse James Freeman's first novel, *Billy Purgatory: I am the Devil Bird*, was released by Booktrope in December of 2011. Under normal circumstances, he writes about skateboards, devil birds, time zombies, emotionally unavailable vampires and Jimmy Hoffa. He's also studied psychology and film and scripted comics. Jesse James lives on a Texas ranch that is haunted by the ghost of LBJ; he is currently writing a Billy Purgatory sequel. When he's not writing books, Jesse James trains falcons to kill leprechaun robots and will continue to do so until the world is relatively safe.

Acknowledgements

Jesse James would like to thank Tess Hardwick, Tracey Hansen, Katherine Fye Sears, Kenneth Shear and Heather Ludviksson for the opportunity to be involved in this project. Oh, and his mom, Debbie, for the opportunity to be involved in any projects at all. Thanks, Mom.

Tracey M. Hansen

Tracey M. Hansen is an author, blogger and procrastinator from Cape Coral, Fla. When she is not making her readers laugh over at www.traceyhansen.com, she likes to travel or hang out at home with her "ManPal" and three feisty fur kids.

Tracey is afraid of flying, the dark, bees and Rosie O'Donnell ... not necessarily in that order. Her goals are to have a restraining order filed against her by a celebrity — and world peace ... in that order.

Tracey went to Catholic school, ~~which explains so much~~.

Inspired by her childhood friend, Holly, who decided to give birth to a daughter diagnosed in utero with both Down Syndrome and a major heart defect, Tracey wrote *Not a Perfect Mom*, which will be published in 2012 by the amazing Booktrope Publishing.

Acknowledgements

To my sister Cindy: Your support and encouragement mean everything to me. To my co-conspirator, Tess Hardwick: Thank you for making all of this possible. Thank you to Katherine Sears at Booktrope for taking a chance on me. Last but not least, to Logan: Words cannot express how proud I am to call you mine. Thank you for always wanting me to succeed. I love you.
—WTYM

Tess Hardwick

Tess Hardwick is a novelist, reader, mommy, wife, daughter, sister and friend — the order of which depends on the day. She is inspired by nature and people and is happiest near or submerged in water. Tess grew up in southern Oregon but now lives in western Washington with her husband and two daughters, Ella, 8, and Emerson, 5, and their puppy, Patches, 8 months.

Her debut novel, *Riversong*, made it to the number 1 Nook Book bestseller slot for a week in October 2011. Since then, she's walked a few inches off the ground, humbled and grateful to have found some commercial success in this precarious and challenging business of selling books. She is currently working on her second and third novels and blogging at www.tesshardwick.com.

When not obsessively working, Tess spends time snuggling with Emerson and helping Ella plan for her future acting career. The rest of her time is happily spent talking on the phone with her mom, drinking too much wine with friends, dancing Zumba and lifting weights over her head in a vain attempt to get rid of the jiggle under her arms. She also attends church, watches movies, reads novels, listens to music, meditates and procrastinates about cooking dinner and doing the laundry.

All of which is possible because of her husband, Dave Hardwick, giver of dreams.

Diane Hughes
Editor

Diane Hughes is a native Tennessean who lives in Nashville. A veteran newspaper writer and editor, she made the natural leap to blogging earlier this year. A born communicator, Diane has quickly learned the quirks of social media and enjoys engaging with her fellow writers online.

She lives with her husband, Michael, with whom she shares a love of photography and the great outdoors. The two of them spend their spare time kayaking, photographing, hiking and backpacking. When she's not hauling a pack into the woods or paddling the rapids on a local creek, Diane finds no greater joy than immersing herself in the pages of a good book. While she has been a reluctant adopter of the e-reader, she is closer than ever to making a Kindle purchase — but swears that she will always prefer the feel of a cold, hard book spine in her hand. Diane blogs at www.dianewordsmith.com and tweets via @dianewordsmith.

Laura Kilmartin

Laura Kilmartin is an attorney who lives in southern Maine and spends her spare time traveling and writing. Laura's contributions to this anthology represent her first professionally published work, but she is shopping for a publisher for her debut novel, *Next Year I'll be Perfect*, in hopes that it will not be her last!

Laura credits her writing success to the love and support of her family and friends. She especially thanks her parents, Mike and Anne Kilmartin, and her sister, Cathy Krusiec, for their ongoing encouragement and enthusiasm. Laura also acknowledges her good fortune in being surrounded by a group of smart, funny and incredibly gifted friends who constantly remind her why she continues to write.

If you liked Laura's essays and want to read more from her view of the world, please visit laurakilmartin.wordpress.com or follow her (elsiekay17) on Twitter.

Marni Mann

A New Englander at heart, Marni Mann, is now a Floridian who finds inspiration in the sandy beaches and hot-pink sunsets of Sarasota. A writer of literary fiction, she taps a mainstream appeal and shakes worldwide taboos, taking her readers on a dark, harrowing and gritty journey. When she's not nose deep in her laptop, she's scouring for chocolate, traveling, reading or walking her four-legged children. Her debut novel, Memoirs Aren't Fairytales, was released in December 2011.

Dedication

For those of you who need hope, who need someone to strike a match because the light has gone out and who have survived cancer, these essays are for you. You're my inspiration. You're the reason I Write For The Fight. Nina Kesner, I remember the day you were diagnosed with breast cancer. One of the happiest moments of my life was when you told us you were in remission. I'm honored to be a part of this project because of survivors like you. I love you.

Acknowledgments

Thank you to Katherine Sears, Ken Shear, Tess Hardwick, Tracey Hansen, Heather Ludviksson, Diane Hughes and Greg Simanson for making this possible, for believing in this great cause and for allowing me to be a part of it.

Karla J. Nellenbach

When she's not writing, Karla Nellenbach enjoys taking a beat-down from that evil invention commonly known as the treadmill, drooling over Sam & Dean Winchester and losing herself in a really good book.

Owned by one very ancient, very fat cat (whose purr machine is in serious need of a muffler) and two rather large, scary-looking dogs (who are afraid of their own shadows — not to mention the neighbor's Yorkie), Karla resides in the land of eternal sunshine that she affectionately refers to as the Seventh Circle of Hell, which can actually be a lovely place to visit from time to time — as long as you remember to bring sunblock.

Karla blogs at karlanellenbach-lastword.blogspot.com and tweets via @LastWord0524.

Terry Persun

Terry Persun has been writing and publishing for more than 25 years. He has published six novels in a variety of genres, including science fiction, mainstream, historical and literary. His work has won the Star of Washington Award, the POW Award for Best Fiction and was a runner-up for the ForeWord Magazine Book of the Year Award. His novels have been published through small, independent publishers for years.

Also a poet, Terry has published two full-length poetry collections and six poetry chapbooks. His short stories and poems have appeared in the *Wisconsin Review, Oracle, Yarrow, Riverrun, NEBO, Oyez Review, Starsong, Hiram Poetry Review, Owen Wister Review, Late Knocking, Kansas Quarterly, Rag Mag, Main Street Rag* and many others.

Terry owns and operates a PR/advertising agency for high-tech companies. His technical articles are published monthly in national and international trade journals. Additionally, Terry and his business partner, Bruce Wiebusch, publish a trade magazine, *Entertainment Engineering*, about the technologies used behind the scenes of movies, theme parks, concerts, etc.

You can find Terry online at www.TerryPersun.com as well as on Amazon, Barnes & Noble and Smashwords.

Bea Thompson
Cover artist

Bea Thompson is an award-winning watercolorist who grew up in Chula Vista, Calif., and earned a Bachelor of Arts degree from San Diego State University. In 1968, Bea and her husband, Ron, a teacher, moved to the Hoopa Indian Reservation in Northern California. Six years later, the family relocated to Selma, Ore., where Bea still lives today and resides in the same house. She and Ron have three children: a stock portfolio manager, a novelist and a musician. In 1994, Bea broke her neck in a car accident and now uses a wheelchair.

A lover of flowers, Bea finds inspiration in their natural rhythms and gestures and allows them to guide the organization of her compositions. Because of the interesting shapes and lines made by their leaves and flowers, Bea's favorites are tulips, irises and lilies. This book's cover art is an example of her newer, lighter, brighter and more transparent palette. Bea has been a member of the Watercolor Society of Oregon since 1984 and exhibits her work at the Southern Oregon Guild in Kerby, Ore.

Laura Tiberio

Laura lives in Seattle, Wash., with her home-remodel-happy husband, three energetic children and one very old cat.

Laura has worked in a variety of professions, ranging from movie theatre management to medical clinics. She currently teaches childbirth and family education in the Ballard area. In her spare time, Laura enjoys camping and exploring the great outdoors with her family, reading both adult and children's fiction, dinner parties where adults drink wine and kids run amok, and belly dancing.

Laura has been writing a diary/memoir of her life and family for the last few years and has attended several writing courses and workshops. In addition to her introspective writings, she is a member of the Society of Children's Book Writers and Illustrators and earned one of 20 "Most Promising Works in Progress" awards at the 2011 SCBWI Western Washington Regional Conference. Laura is currently working on a variety of middle-grade novels and the occasional picture book.

Acknowledgements

Laura would like to thank her family and friends for their support of her writing ventures — both by reading her work and watching her kids so that she could attend meetings, classes and critique groups. Laura dedicates her essays in this anthology to the countless women and their families who are fighting for their lives every day. And to her grandmothers, who both survived breast cancer.

Laura Zera

Laura Zera has lived and worked in Canada, South Africa and Cameroon; she now makes her home in Seattle, Wash., where she is currently working on her second book, a memoir about being raised by a schizophrenic mother. Laura's first book (written as Laura Enridge), 2004's Tro-tros and Potholes, chronicles her solo adventures through five countries of West Africa. Follow her on Twitter @laurazera and visit her blog at laurazera.com.

Dedication

I am honored to be one of the authors included in this book. I am also lucky that the number of people in my life who have been diagnosed with breast cancer has been small. Their journeys, however, are not. They managed, and still manage, to amaze and inspire me with their bravery and resilience. To all of those who must take such a journey, you are heroes and warriors in the truest sense.

JUN 14 2013

PORTLAND PUBLIC LIBRARY SYSTEM
5 MONUMENT SQUARE
PORTLAND, ME 04101

WITHDRAWN

16826439R00106

Made in the USA
Lexington, KY
13 August 2012